# *Creative*
# FINISHING TOUCHES
# WITH FABRIC

Cover pictures: (l) Eaglemoss/Steve Tanner; (tr) Marie Claire
Idées/C. Fleurent/C. Lancrenon; (br) IPC Magazines/
Robert Harding Syndication/Trevor Richards.

Page 1: IPC Magazines/Robert Harding Syndication/
Simon Brown; page 3 Modes et Travaux/J.L.Scotto; page 4
Marie Claire Idées/Hussenot/Chastres/Lancrenon; page 5
Eaglemoss/Steve Tanner.

Based on *Creating Your Home,*
published in the UK by
© Eaglemoss Publications Ltd 1996
All rights reserved

First published in North America
in 1997 by Betterway Books,
an imprint of F&W Publications Inc.
1507 Dana Avenue
Cincinnati, Ohio 45207
1-800/289-0963

ISBN 1-55870-451-5

Manufactured in Hong Kong

10 9 8 7 6 5 4 3 2 1

# *Creative*
# FINISHING TOUCHES
# WITH FABRIC

BETTERWAY BOOKS

# Contents

## SPICE UP YOUR DINING ROOM

## PERSONALIZE YOUR HOME WITH FABRIC FLOURISHES

# FABRIC-COVERED FURNITURE

*Cover furniture with fabric as a stylish way to coordinate occasional pieces with a colour scheme and soft furnishings. Self-assembly furniture with straight and simple lines is perfect for this treatment.*

Fabric-covered furniture provides a most convenient way to complement different colour and pattern elements in a room. Easy on the eye, the advantage of its subtle, low-key image is the visual balance it can help maintain within a scheme. Covered in fabric to match or coordinate with curtains or chair covers, these pieces look stylish in their own right and blend with the surroundings.

This unobtrusive quality can be a very useful ploy if you want to incorporate a piece such as a table or a chest of drawers into a scheme where a particular furniture style or wood colour is established, and another addition would be overpowering, or is simply not

a realistic proposition. Fabric coverings are also a good way to improve on basic-looking shelves and cupboards or to minimize the bulk of a chest of drawers, where you can simply cover the drawer fronts with fabric.

The technique itself is relatively straightforward. Initially, the furniture is coated with PVA adhesive, and wrapped with an interlining fabric which provides a cushioned base for the main fabric cover. The process is simplified if you use flat-pack furniture, as you can cover each piece before assembly. For ease, choose furniture with straight, square-section legs and shelves with deep edges which show off the fabric to advantage.

*Covering furniture with fabric to match the rest of the scheme is an impressive treatment for reviving an old piece, like this table for example, or a clever way to give a new look to plain flat-pack designs.*

# COVERING A TABLE

These instructions are for covering a square-legged self-assembly table, of the type available from furniture super-stores. The top and legs are covered with fabric before final assembly. The interlining is butt joined to produce a closely fitting 'second skin' with no tell-tale seams.

Choose a closely woven, mediumweight fabric such as glazed cotton, and avoid fabrics which fray easily. Patterned fabrics make an especially dramatic impact. As when covering any piece of furniture that will be viewed from all sides, choose a fabric without a strongly directional pattern, as this could look odd when viewed the wrong way up. As a practical measure, have a glass top cut to fit the table.

Although not essential, you can make a paper pattern to ensure accurate cutting of the main fabric. To do this, re-measure the table after the interlining is fitted. Before cutting out the main fabric, make sure that the ends of the fabric are at right angles to the selvedges, then cut off the selvedges. Iron all the fabrics to remove creases.

Work on a large flat surface such as a kitchen table, and cover it with a protective plastic sheet.

## MEASURING FOR FABRIC

*Assessing the fabric width:* Depending on the size and shape of the table, and the fabric design, you can lay the fabric lengthways or widthways over the table. Here, one fabric width covers the table length. Estimate the minimum fabric width needed by measuring the length of the table (**A**). Allow an extra 1.5cm (⅝in) for turnings on each side.

*For the table top:* Measure the table top width (**B**). Double it and add twice the depth of the sides (**C**) plus 3cm (1¼in) for turnings and overlaps at the ends. Cut a piece to this length. Also include two fabric strips to cover the table top ends, to measure **B** x **C** plus a 1.5cm (⅝in) allowance all round.

*For the table legs:* Measure round a leg (**D**) and add 3cm (1¼in) for turnings. Measure the length of the leg (**E**) and add 3cm (1¼in) at each end. You need four pieces of fabric **D** x **E** for the legs.

*For interlining:* Measure up for the interlining in the same way, but omit extra fabric for turnings.

### YOU WILL NEED

- ❖ SELF-ASSEMBLY TABLE
- ❖ MAIN FABRIC
- ❖ INTERLINING (bump or domette)
- ❖ PVA ADHESIVE (two 21 fl oz packs are sufficient to interline and cover an average-sized occasional table)
- ❖ LARGE MIXING BOWL
- ❖ PAPER for patterns (optional)
- ❖ FELT for leg bases
- ❖ DRESSMAKING PINS AND SCISSORS
- ❖ DRESSMAKERS' MARKER PEN
- ❖ DECORATORS' 40mm (1½in) PAINT BRUSH
- ❖ KITCHEN PAPER
- ❖ IRON AND PROTECTIVE CLOTH
- ❖ PLASTIC SHEETING
- ❖ GLASS TABLE TOP (optional)

**1** **Preparing the adhesive** Squeeze half the contents of one adhesive pack into the mixing bowl and add a little cold water to make a thick, creamy consistency. Stir well. Keep it covered and mix more adhesive in the same way when needed.

**2** **Interlining the table top** With the table top right side up, brush adhesive evenly over the top and sides. Lay the interlining over it, lining it up with the lower back edge and leaving an overhang at each end. Smooth and press the interlining flat to stick, paying particular attention to the edges.

**3** **Shaping the corners** Snip the overhang at each corner. Press the fabric to the sides and ends. Trim the excess at the corners and both ends, level with the lower edge.

**4** **Interlining the base** Turn the table top over, coat the base with adhesive and press the interlining in place. Trim it level with the sides and ends. Leave to dry.

**5** **Interlining the table legs** Cover each leg with adhesive and wrap the interlining round, trimming to butt join it along one long edge. Smooth it flat to fit tightly, then trim it level at the top and base of the leg. Leave to dry.

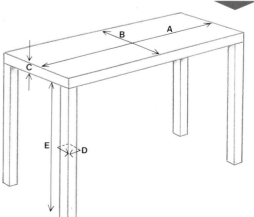

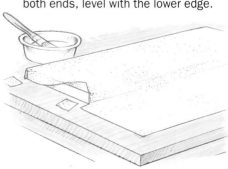

*Glazed cotton toile de Jouy is an attractive option for fabric-covered furniture. The figurative designs associated with these fabrics have a clarity and impact that complement the simple lines of each piece.*

**7 Covering the table** Brush adhesive over the top, including the fabric overlaps at the sides. Spread adhesive along the short edges and one long edge on the wrong side of the main fabric. Turn under 1.5cm (⅝in) on these edges and press. Place the fabric so that its sides are level with the table ends and the long, raw end overlaps the base edge. Smooth to stick. Turn the table over. Spread adhesive over the base and press the long overlap flat. Smooth the remaining fabric flat. Leave to dry.

**8 Covering the legs** Brush adhesive over each leg. Spread adhesive along one long edge and the short edges on the wrong side of the main fabric. Turn under 1.5cm (⅝in) and press to form a neat edge. Position the fabric with the raw edge overlap along one long edge and wrap the fabric round. Spread adhesive over the wrong side of the turned edge and press it flat.

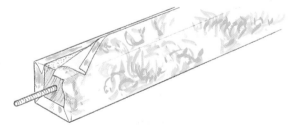

**9 Neatening the leg ends** At the screw end, brush the fabric overlap with adhesive and fold it round the end, trimming excess as necessary. At the foot end, brush the overlaps with adhesive and fold the fabric underneath. When dry, neaten with a square of felt.

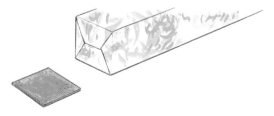

**6 Covering the table ends** Brush adhesive evenly over the interlining on the two ends of the table top and over the adjacent surfaces by 1.5cm (⅝in) to hold the overlaps. Press the main fabric end pieces down smoothly. Stretch the corner point over along the top edge and neatly fold in the flaps at each side, applying more adhesive as necessary to hold them flat. Repeat top and bottom at each corner.

**10 Assembling the table** When the fabrics are dry, check the edges are firmly stuck. Turn the table upside down. Pierce the screw holes and twist each leg in place, with the fabric joins facing inwards. Add a glass top if desired.

# FABRIC-COVERED SHELVES

You can cover shelves in a similar way to a table top. The deeper the shelf, the more effective the fabric will be. If you are planning to cover a stack of shelves with a patterned fabric, position the fabric so that the design repeat is shown to advantage across the front of the shelves. As with tables, pre-covering them with interlining will give a more sumptuous, finished look.

Use the same basic materials listed and methods as for *Covering a Table*.

**Shelves with visible supports** As for step 6, *Covering a Table*, cover the short ends of the shelf first before wrapping the fabric round the whole shelf. Arrange the join along the lower back edge of the shelf. If the supports are simple wooden shapes, you can also cover these with fabric.

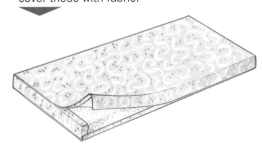

**Shelves with hidden supports** Some shelves are supported on rods which fit into holes drilled in the back of the shelf. First remove the support rods and cover the short ends of the shelves as before. Then wrap the fabric over the top, front edge and underside of the shelf, turning 1.5cm (⅝in) under on the back edge at both ends. Allow for side turnings as before. Re-insert the rod supports when the fabric is firmly fixed and dry.

**Recessed shelves** It is not necessary to cover the short ends on shelves to be fitted in a recess. When cutting fabric to cover a recessed shelf, allow for turnings at the side edges as before, for a neat finish.

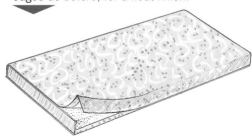

*◀ Fabric-covered shelves can look as interesting as the objects placed on them. For maximum impact choose a fabric to coordinate with the wallcovering and complement the colours of the ornaments.*

*▼ For any chest of drawers that may have seen better days, covering the drawer fronts with fabric gives more scope than paint – it's also a clever way to disguise any minor faults in the wood. Here a range of blue dress cotton prints provide a pattern theme that's echoed in the rest of the scheme.*

# SLIP-OVER FOOTSTOOL COVERS

*When a footstool has a slip-over cover, you can sit down,
put your feet up and relax, confident that while it suits the room to perfection,
the cover is also easy to remove for cleaning.*

Footstools in a variety of shapes and sizes offer a comfy resting place for weary feet and provide flexible additional seating. Light and mobile, they can be carried from room to room with ease, or stored under chairs ready for use.

Traditionally, footstools are manufactured in the same way as chairs, with an upholstered core and fixed cover. Making a slip-over cover for the stool protects the original top fabric from wear and dirt or disguises an already worn appearance. A coordinated cover can also link the stool in with a new colour scheme or ensure its general neutrality.

You can tailor the cover to the shape of the stool, defining the outline with piping, braids or frills in matching or contrasting fabrics and make a plain or shaped edge. The cover just slides over the existing stool top and pulls down firmly in position.

Like loose covers, you can make a slip-over footstool cover in cotton furnishing fabric or a lightweight upholstery fabric to fit in with the existing soft furnishings in the room. As you only need a small amount of fabric, it's an ideal opportunity to use up some of those fabric remnants you have left over from previous soft furnishing projects. For fun, you can mix and match a variety of plain and printed fabrics together in one cover.

*For a truly sophisticated effect, a slip-over cover for a footstool is made in a colour-coordinated, hardwearing cotton fabric to match the stylish lambrequin window dressing.*

# MAKING A FRILLED COVER

In making this slip-over cover, you fuse a layer of lightweight wadding to the wrong side of the fabric to give the top body, and apply interfacing round the side for a crisp finish. Aim to centre pattern motifs round the side drop and position a large motif in the centre of the top circle. Piping the top edge of the cover defines the shape of the stool, while a gathered frill in a coordinating print decorates the hem. As an alternative to iron-on wadding and interfacing, you can substitute an interlining fabric, such as bump or domette, tacked to the wrong side of the fabric (except the frill).

> ## YOU WILL NEED
> ❖ FURNISHING FABRIC in three coordinating prints
> ❖ IRON-ON WADDING
> ❖ MEDIUMWEIGHT IRON-ON INTERFACING
> ❖ PIPING CORD AND COVERING FABRIC
> ❖ MATCHING SEWING THREAD

**1 Cutting the circular top**
Measure the diameter of the stool top. Cut out one circle of fabric to this size, adding a 1.5cm (⅝in) seam allowance all round. Use this fabric piece as a pattern to cut one piece of iron-on wadding. Fuse to the wrong side of the fabric.

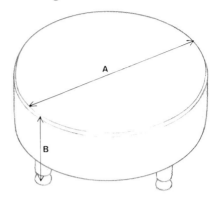

**2 Measuring the side**
Measure the depth of the stool side, from top to feet, and deduct 6cm (2½in) to allow for a frill. Centring any motifs, cut one fabric strip to the circumference of the stool top by the chosen depth, adding 1.5cm (⅝in) all round for seams. Use this piece as a pattern to cut out a strip of interfacing. Fuse the interfacing to the wrong side of the fabric strip.

◢ *Four coordinating fabrics are teamed together to make this charming little footstool cover. This happy mix-and-match of designs shows how effective this approach can be and how you can put remnants to good use.*

**3 Adding the piping** Make up sufficient fabric-covered piping to go all round the outer edge of the top, plus 2.5cm (1in) for overlaps. Matching raw edges, pin and tack piping all round the right side of top, clipping into the seam allowance if necessary. Join ends of piping together to fit.

**4 Assembling the cover** With right sides together, pin and stitch the short ends of the side piece together. Trim and press seam open. With right sides together, matching raw edges, pin and stitch the side piece to the top cover, over piping. Remove tacking and neaten raw edges.

**5 Cutting the frill** Measure the circumference of the side and double the measurement. Cut 8cm (3¼in) wide strips across the fabric width to this measurement. Make up into a circular folded frill, with two rows of gathering stitches along the raw edges.

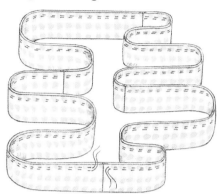

**6 Attaching the frill** Fold the side piece and frill into quarters and mark the folds with pins. With right sides together and aligning raw edges, place frill to hem edge of side. Match marker pins, pulling up the gathering stitches on the frill evenly to fit. Stitch in place. Remove gathering stitches. Neaten raw edges. Slip cover over stool and ease to shape. If necessary, iron the cover on the stool.

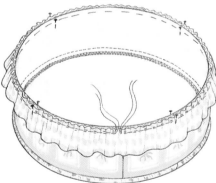

# T I P

### REVERSIBLE COVER

Make up two simple stool covers in contrasting fabrics, leaving an opening in the top seam on one cover. Place the covers with right sides together; join round the base edge. Turn the cover to the right side through the opening. Turn in opening edges and slipstitch together. As a final touch, you can stitch a double braid trim round the base.

◣ *Echo the modern setting with a slip-over stool cover in plain yellow, keeping the design plain to match the chaise longue. Position a layer of wadding behind the stool top to give a slightly rounded crown and topstitch on either side of each seam and round the hem to give a tailored finish.*

# REVERSED SCALLOP STOOL TOP

A charming celestial fabric dotted with suns and stars makes a great pull-on cover for a small footstool. Hand sew a little bell to the point of each cut-out scallop shape for an amusing finishing touch.

**1** **Cutting out top** Measure the diameter of the stool top. Cut out one circle of fabric to this size, adding 1.5cm (⅝in) seam allowances all round the outer edge. Use this fabric piece as a pattern to cut one circle from iron-on interfacing. Fuse to the wrong side of the fabric. Measure the depth of the stool and decide on the cover length.

☑ *Hanging bells add a jolly touch to this cover. The reverse scallops reveal the stool's toning stripes.*

**2** **Making inverted scallop template** To find the size of the inverted scallops, measure round the circumference of the stool top and divide it into seven equal sections. To make a template for the scallop, draw a circle on a sheet of paper with the diameter of one-seventh the circumference of the stool. Mark across the centre of the circle (**A**). Draw a straight vertical line on each side to the depth of the cover (**B**) and join at the top with a horizontal line.

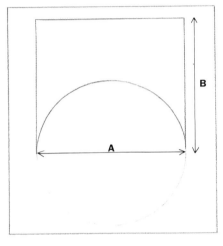

**3** **Cutting out the pattern** Cut a piece of paper the length of the stool circumference by the chosen depth. Use the scallop template to mark seven scallops along one edge of the pattern piece. Cut out the pattern.

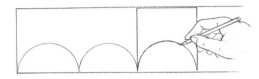

**4** **Cutting out side pieces** Use the pattern to cut one piece from fabric and one piece from lining fabric, adding 1.5cm (⅝in) seam allowances all round.

**5** **Making up side section** With right sides together, stitch ends of side piece together. Repeat for lining. Place fabric to lining with right sides facing; pin and stitch round the scalloped edge. Clip into curves and trim close to the stitching round the scallops. Turn right side out and press. Turn 1.5cm (⅝in) in along the top edge of main fabric and lining and press.

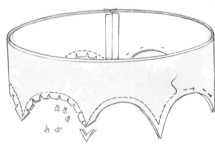

**6** **Stitch top to side** Stitch round top circle just inside seamline, 1.5cm (⅝in) from the edge. Snip into edge close to stitching at 2.5cm (1in) intervals. Slip top circle between folded edges of side piece, with folded edges just covering the stitches; pin then topstitch in place all round top.

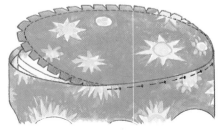

**7** **Adding decoration** Hand sew a little bell (or substitute a tassel or other suitable trimming) to each scallop point. Slide cover over top of stool.

# CONTOURED SEAT LININGS

*Make plain wicker and wooden seating comfortable with fitted padded linings and squashy cushions. Choose eye-catching fabrics for covers that look inviting whether you're sitting indoors or out.*

Traditional wicker chairs and wooden benches have the kind of basic good looks and low-key styling that make them a practical option for informal seating, whether the setting is indoors or out. Always a classic choice for conservatories and sunny terraces, they are also a marvellous way to create a relaxed, garden room atmosphere far from a real garden.

Wherever this furniture is used, you can enhance its comfortable image by making made-to-measure padded linings and fitted cushions. Most linings are anchored by a plump cushion, or held in place with touch-and-close tape or fabric ties. Besides being easily washable, removable linings also offer opportunities for quick cover changes when you want to create a different mood with new fabric covers as the seasons change.

Large wicker armchairs and wooden benches are relatively inexpensive to buy and are easy to maintain. Padded linings can really rejuvenate these old pieces too. You can find secondhand bargains which, after a good wash and brush-up or a quick coat of spray paint or wood stain, can look very attractive. Choose robust fabrics that can withstand the wear and tear of indoor and outdoor life. For the most harmonious effects, select plains, stripes or florals that complement the natural look of wicker and wood.

*Smart green stripes are a classic fabric choice for conservatory seating. Here, they are used to advantage to follow the generous lines of this wicker chair. Matching binding, piping and small, self-covered buttons add design style and neat finishing touches.*

# MAKING A CONTOURED CHAIR LINING

The following steps are for a piped, padded lining and seat cushion for a wicker chair. The lining covers the entire inside area of the chair, and is held in place by the deep seat cushion. The cushion cover is made in two pieces with a central piped seam and gently gathered 'Turkish' corners. For easy fitting over the thick foam pad, allow for the opening zip on the cushion cover to extend round both back corners.

As a finishing touch and for optimum comfort, prop a matching fabric scatter cushion at the back of the chair.

When cutting out the fabrics, add 1.5cm (⅝in) round each pattern edge for seams.

To reduce fabric costs, you can use a different, less expensive fabric for the underside of the chair lining if desired, but make sure it tones with the main fabric.

## MAKING THE CHAIR LINING

**1 Making the back pattern** Place a large sheet of paper over the inside of the chair back and arms and tape it to hold. Mould the paper round the curves and contours, pinning out darts in the back corners where necessary to achieve a flat finish. Remove the pattern from the chair. Mark the darts and cut out round the outer edges. Replace the pattern and check its fit.

**2 Making the base pattern** Smooth a sheet of paper over the chair seat as for the back. Mark round the outer edge of the seat. Remove the paper and cut it out along the marked line. Replace the pattern to check its fit. Place the back and base patterns into the chair and check that they fit together, making any adjustments as needed.

**3 Cutting out the lining** Use the patterns to cut out two back and two base linings from fabric, adding the seam allowances all round. Pin and stitch any darts in both back pieces, tapering them into a point and pressing them towards the centre. Measure along the top and side edges of the back lining to estimate the length of piping cord and fabric required for covered piping, and prepare covered piping to this length.

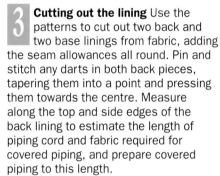

**4 Assembling the top lining** With right sides together, stitch the piping to one back lining piece, tapering the ends into the seam allowance at the front edges. With right sides together, join the back to the piped base lining piece.

**5 Completing the lining** Pin and stitch the remaining back and base linings together. With the top and underside linings right sides together, pin and stitch all round, catching in the piping and leaving a central opening in the seam. Trim and turn right side out.

**6 Fitting the foam** Use the back pattern to cut one piece from 5cm (2in) thick foam; do not add any seam allowance. Ease the foam into the back lining. Turn in and slipstitch the opening closed. To stop the foam from slipping out of place, slipstitch along the seat seam through all layers. Fit the lining into the chair.

## MAKING THE SEAT CUSHION

**1 Preparing the foam** Make a paper pattern for the foam as for *Making the Chair Lining step 2*, but shorten the length by 5cm (2in) to allow for the padded lining. Place the pattern on the 12.5cm (5in) thick foam, draw around it and cut out along the marked line.

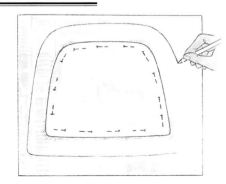

**2 Adding the gusset allowance** Pin the foam pattern on to a new sheet of paper. Measure the depth of the foam, halve this measurement and add on 1.5cm (⅝in) for seams. This should give 7.75cm (3⅛in). Mark this distance away from the foam pattern all round. Measure this outer line to estimate for piping cord. Cut out the pattern and use it to cut out two pieces from fabric; remember the seam allowance is included in the pattern.

**Shaping front corners** Mark 9cm (3½in) on either side of each front corner on one cushion piece. Place a saucer between the marks and draw round in a curve. Trim the marked lines. Use to shape the other cover piece.

**Creating Turkish corners** Run a row of gathering stitches round the curved edge of each front corner. Pull up the gathers evenly to shape, and fasten off the threads securely.

△ *This delicately drawn strawberry print, chosen for the comfortably padded lining and cushions on this wicker chair, has all the fresh, summery appeal that's associated with indoor-outdoor living.*

**Adding the piping and zip** Stitch covered piping to the right side of one cushion piece, beginning and ending at the centre back. Measure and mark the zip position centrally along one back edge. With right sides together, pin and tack the cushion pieces together up to the zip marks. Machine stitch along the piping stitching line. Fit the zip. Remove the tacking stitches, turn right side out and insert the foam pad.

# PADDED BENCH LINER

This lightweight bench liner is padded with several layers of wadding. Buttons quilt the layers together and fabric ties secure the liner to the bench; alternatively, substitute straps with touch-and-close tab fastenings.

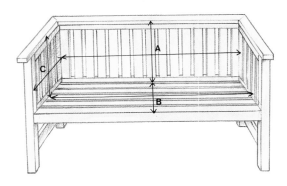

## YOU WILL NEED

❖ PATTERN PAPER, TAPE MEASURE AND SAUCER
❖ MAIN FABRIC
❖ LIGHTWEIGHT, 50gm (2oz) WADDING
❖ UPHOLSTERY WEIGHT, 300gm (12oz) WADDING
❖ MATCHING SEWING THREADS
❖ COVERED PIPING CORD
❖ MACHINE ZIP OR PIPING FOOT
❖ SHANKED BUTTONS, STRONG THREAD

**1 Making a pattern** Measure the inside seat back width and height **(A)**, the inside seat length and depth **(B)** and the inside side depth and height **(C)**. Transfer these sizes to paper, adding 1.5cm (⅝in) all round for seams. Use a saucer to shape curves on the front corners of **B** and **C** patterns. Cut out the patterns. Fit them on the bench and mark on appropriate positions for ties.

**2 Preparing the fabrics** *For the cover:* From fabric and lightweight wadding, cut out two **A**, two **B** and four **C** panels. With fabric wrong side down, pin each panel over a matching wadding piece and tack edges. *For the ties:* From fabric cut out 10 strips, 66 x 9cm (26 x 3½in) (or the number required). *For the padded inserts:* Trim off the seam allowance round each pattern. Then, from upholstery wadding cut two **A**, two **B** and four **C** panels. *For piping:* Measure all round the outside edge of the liner panels and prepare piping to this length.

**3 Assembling the panels** With right sides together and raw edges level, join one **C** panel to each side of one **A** panel and join **A** to **B**. Press seams open and trim excess wadding. Stitch piping round the edge, clipping to ease into curves. Join the underside panels in the same way, but when joining **A** to **B**, stitch for 9cm (3½in) only at each side.

**4 Making the ties** With right sides together, fold each strip in half along its length. Machine stitch the seam and turn right side out. Turn in and stitch ends closed. Fold each tie in half across its width and pin and stitch in place on the liner underside. Pin the tie ends flat to the liner to prevent them catching in the next sewing stage.

**5 Assembling the liner** With right sides together and raw edges level, pin and stitch the top to the underside, stitching along the piping stitching line. Remove tacking, clip curves and excess wadding and turn right side out. To insert the wadding, place the upholstery wadding panels together in pairs. Lay the liner flat with underside up, and ease the wadding pairs into place through the back opening. Smooth into the corners. Slipstitch the opening closed.

**6 Button quilting the liner** Lay the liner flat, top side up. Use pins to mark the chosen button positions, spacing them at regular intervals to secure the layers. Use strong thread to stitch each button from shank to shank through all thicknesses.

◀ *This bench, with its colourful vegetable print lining, will make any room feel like a sunny garden.*

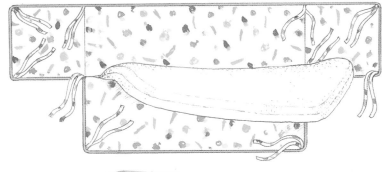

# APPLIQUE CUSHION COVERS

*Decorate plain fabric scatter cushions with motifs cut
from a favourite fabric. Light padding under each motif gives the
cushions a softly quilted look.*

Whenever you buy or make a new pair of living room curtains you are likely to want new cushions to match. Appliqué cushions are a stylish option and, because you are using a plain fabric for the main part of the cushion, relatively inexpensive.

To make an appliqué cushion you simply cut out motifs from a remnant of fabric, for example your curtain fabric, and stitch them on to a plain fabric background. As a precaution, make sure you can care for both fabrics in the same way. If you already have some suitable plain fabric cushions, you can appliqué directly on to these.

Many current fabric designs printed with large floral, fruit or animal motifs are perfect for appliqué. Look for fabric with strong, clear images with well defined outlines, as these are easy to cut out and stitch.

The cushions shown here are decorated with fruit shapes cut from a fruit-patterned fabric. To give the fruits a plump look, they are backed with polyester wadding before being stitched to the cushions.

*Rosy apples, blushing pears and ripe lemons look resplendent on their flame-coloured backgrounds. A layer of wadding under each fruit shape emphasizes its softly rounded form.*

19

# FRUIT CUSHION COVERS

## YOU WILL NEED

*For cover 40cm/16in square*

- ❖ PLAIN FURNISHING FABRIC 80cm (⅞yd) for the cushion cover and piping
- ❖ FRUIT-PRINT FABRIC
- ❖ PLAIN COTTON FABRIC for backing the motifs
- ❖ PIPING CORD 1.8m (1⅞yd)
- ❖ LIGHTWEIGHT POLYESTER WADDING 50g (2oz)
- ❖ MACHINE EMBROIDERY THREAD in colours to match the motifs
- ❖ SEWING THREAD to match the plain fabric

These steps show how to make appliqué cushions with a piped edge and a back-vent opening. They are decorated on the front with appliquéd fabric fruits and leaves, padded with wadding.

## T I P

### ABSTRACT SHAPES

If you have used a mini-print, striped or checked fabric for your curtains, you can appliqué strips, squares, triangles and other shapes on to the cushion instead of printed motifs.

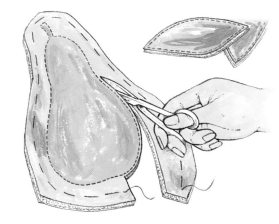

**Placing the motifs** Position the motifs on the cushion front, moving them around until you are happy with the effect. You may want to overlap the motifs in places. Pin, then tack them in place.

**Zigzag stitching** Set your machine to an open zigzag stitch and, using matching thread, stitch around the first motif. Reset the machine to a close zigzag and stitch around the motif again. Pull the threads through to the back of the work and fasten them off. Change the thread to match the remaining motifs and stitch them in the same way.

**Attaching the piping** Make up 1.8m (1⅞yd) of fabric-covered piping. With raw edges matching, pin and tack the piping around the right side of the cover front, clipping into the seam allowances at the corners so they lie flat and neatly joining the ends.

**Making up the cover** On one long edge of each back rectangle, turn under a 5mm (¼in) then a 1cm (⅜in) hem and machine stitch. With right sides together and raw edges matching, lay the back pieces over the front so the hemmed edges overlap. Pin, tack and stitch the outer edge taking a 1.5cm (⅝in) seam. Trim the corners, turn the cover right side out and press it. Insert the pad.

**Cutting out** From the plain fabric cut one 43cm (17¼in) square for the cushion front and two 43 x 30cm (17¼ x 12in) rectangles for the back. Measurements include a 1.5cm (⅝in) seam allowance.

**Preparing the motifs** Decide which motifs to use and roughly cut them out, leaving a 5cm (2in) border all round. Cut a piece of wadding and plain fabric to the same size as each motif, and sandwich the wadding between the two fabric pieces, right sides out. Tack round the edges. Machine stitch around the edge of each motif. Cut around the motif 3mm (⅛in) outside the stitching.

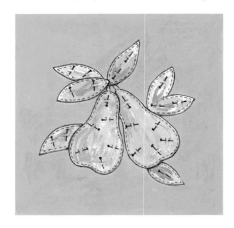

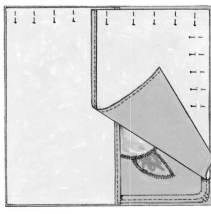

*To help you plan your appliqué designs, cut out a broad selection of fruit motifs from your fabric and group them in different ways until you find an arrangement you like for each cushion.*

# FELT APPLIQUE

*Cleverly cut felt provides exotic swirls of colourful appliqué on cushions and throws. Choose bold symmetrical patterns and simply topstitch the felt in place.*

F elt is an ideal appliqué fabric – not only does it come in a wonderful array of colours, but it doesn't fray when cut. Felt is made from bonded fibres so there is no grain or right and wrong side, making it particularly easy to work with. It's the perfect choice for intricate appliqué designs like the ones shown here, as there is no need for fiddly hemming of edges.

The only drawback is that felt does not wash well, but you can take the finished appliquéd cushions and throw to be professionally dry-cleaned when needed.

You can buy felt in small squares or by the metre (yard) for larger projects. For the cushion or throw background fabric, choose a cloth with a similar feel to felt, such as a light to mediumweight wool or brushed cotton. The fabric needs to have sufficient body to hold the appliqué without puckering.

Any colour scheme can be catered to with felt appliqué. Subtle shades, such as white on beige, white on white or an ice-cream pastel mix, enhance a soft muted decor; while bright jewel or tangy acid colours on a white, black or contrast-coloured ground make a strong colour statement in any room. It's a good idea to buy samples and try out a few different colour combinations before making your final fabric choice.

*Non-fraying felt is so easy to work with that you can build up highly intricate appliqué designs with minimal effort. The swirls and scallops of this flamboyant white-on-beige pattern were inspired by the relief designs on the terracotta pots behind.*

# FELT APPLIQUE CUSHIONS

The three appliqué cushion designs featured here have a naive, folksy appeal, enhanced by the choice of a bold coloured felt on a contrasting background. Each design spreads out from the centre in a perfectly symmetrical mirror image. You can enlarge the designs to any size you wish. Define the cushion edges with contrast piping to match the felt appliqué.

**1 Making the pattern** Measure the pad to find the finished cushion size, and cut a tracing paper square to this size. Fold the paper into quarters, crease well, then open it out. Enlarge one of the patterns below to fit easily into one quarter of the paper square. Using a transfer pencil, trace the design into each quarter, with the design lines matching across the creases.

**2 Transferring the design** Cut one square of felt and one of fusible webbing to the same size as the tracing paper pattern. Fuse the webbing to one side of the felt. Lay the pattern over the webbing backing paper and apply a warm iron to transfer the design.

**3 Cutting out the design** Using a sharp pair of scissors, cut out the appliqué design; use small embroidery scissors for any intricate sections.

▶ Bold red felt designs appliquéd on to slate grey backgrounds make for eye-catching, high contrast results on these three cushion covers.

**4 Cutting out the cushion pieces** From the background fabric, cut one cushion front piece the finished size of the cushion plus 1.5cm (⅝in) all round for seams, and one cushion back piece to the size of the front piece plus an extra 2cm (¾in) across the width to allow for inserting the zip. Place the zip one-quarter of the way across the cushion back for easy removal of the pad.

## T I P

### MAKING APPLIQUE PATTERNS

To create your own patterns, cut a square of paper to the chosen finished size of the appliqué. Fold it into quarters, then diagonally to form a triangle. Mark on a pattern with a pencil, then cut it out and unfold the paper. Incorporate extra felt motifs, such as dots, diamonds and swirls, into the design as desired.

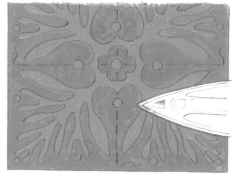

**5 Applying the appliqué** Tack across the cushion front piece through the centre, vertically and horizontally, to provide guidelines. Peel the backing off the fusible webbing and, using the tacked lines as a guide, place the felt appliqué centrally on the cushion front. Fuse in place.

**appliqué quarter patterns**

**6** **Topstitching**
Using sewing thread to match the felt, topstitch close to the edges of the appliqué all round the design. Check the thread tension on fabric scraps before you begin.

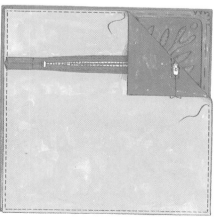

**7** **Finishing the cover**
Pin and tack the piping around the edges of the cushion front, on the right side. Partially open the zip on the back cover piece and lay it over the front, with right sides together. Pin and stitch around the edges. Trim and neaten the seam allowances, turn the cover right side out and insert the pad.

# SCALLOPED THROW

This felt appliqué throw is given added appeal by a dainty scalloped border around the edge. The swirly appliqué motifs were simply drawn freehand on to webbing-backed felt and applied round the edges of the throw in a random pattern. Choose a lightweight woollen blanket or a large piece of lightweight felt as the background fabric.

### YOU WILL NEED

❖ **FABRIC** for throw
❖ **FELT**
❖ **DOUBLE-SIDED FUSIBLE WEBBING (BONDAWEB)**
❖ **TRANSFER PENCIL AND TRACING PAPER**
❖ **CARDBOARD**
❖ **SHARP SCISSORS**
❖ **MATCHING THREADS**

**1** **Enlarging the pattern** Cut the throw fabric to the desired size. Enlarge the corner and random motifs to the required size, to suit the throw's proportions and to ensure the border scallops will fit evenly around the edges. Apply fusible webbing to the back of the felt.

**2** **Transferring the border pattern** Using a transfer pencil and tracing paper, copy the scalloped border on the corner pattern below on to the paper backing four times – once in each corner. Trace the section of scalloped border between the blue lines on to cardboard and cut out to make a template. Use this to mark scallops out from each corner section in a straight line; there probably won't be room to mark all the scallops for each throw edge in one go, so mark additional rows as needed, to butt join.

**3** **Transferring the main pattern** Use tracing paper and a transfer pencil to copy the corner motif on to the backing paper four times. Transfer the random motifs in the same way, repeating them as many times as desired and supplementing them with freehand motifs of your own if you wish.

◢ *Work a felt appliqué throw in white on white for an elegantly understated effect; the subtle variations in tone and texture are all the contrast you need.*

**4** **Fusing the shapes** Cut out the shapes. Fuse the border in place around the throw edges, butting together any joins. Lay the throw flat and arrange the corner motifs and other shapes on it. When happy with the arrangement, fuse in place.

**5** **Trimming the edge** Topstitch the border and shapes in place around all edges, using thread in the machine needle to match the felt, and thread in the bobbin to match the backing fabric. Trim the throw fabric level with the scalloped border's outer edge.

**random motifs**

**corner motif**

**scalloped border**

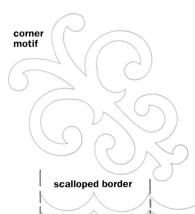

# WOVEN RIBBON CUSHIONS

*Weave a collection of brilliantly coloured ribbons together to create sumptuous cushion designs. Framed with colour-matched fabrics or decorated with embroidery stitches, they look unashamedly opulent.*

R ibbon weaving is a really versatile technique which can be adapted to suit any furnishing style. Designs can be worked in simple basket weave or in more complex styles – forming patchwork squares or zigzags, for example. With all these techniques the results are quick, and effects can be dramatically different depending on your choice of ribbons. These are available in so many colours, finishes and widths that you can create pattern effects ranging from bold multi-coloured plaids in velvet and taffeta to mini-designs in pretty pastel satins, all using the same weaving technique.

Ribbon weaving is worked by pinning lines of ribbon to a soft board. The pins keep the ribbon taut, and a backing fabric, placed under the ribbons,

acts as a stabilizing layer for the finished weave. The warp is created by pinning ribbons vertically side by side; the weft is made up of ribbons woven in and out across these lines to form the design. The design can be altered at any time during this process simply by changing the ribbon sequence or weaving over the top with narrower ribbons for textural interest.

There are no set rules for combining ribbons together in a design, apart from choosing colourfast ribbons if the cushion is to be laundered. Some successful designs are often achieved unexpectedly by trying out different arrangements, although it's helpful to work with a preliminary sketch of a design, especially when estimating for ribbon quantities, and when weaving to a set colour sequence.

*The distinctive chequered cushion on the left is created by weaving together richly coloured ribbons in a classic basket weave formation. Embroidered stars, worked in contrasting shades at the corners of the ribbon squares, add textural interest.*

# Basket Weave Cushion Panel

Woven ribbon panels make splendid centrepieces for cushions of all sizes. You can enlarge the panel with a fabric border to accommodate the cushion pad size or to act as a flattering frame for the design. Options include a small jewel-bright panel set into a deep border for maximum impact, or you can use wide ribbons to weave a large-scale design and frame it with a narrow border. Alternatively, weave the panel to fit the entire cushion front, and embellish it with embroidery stitches in contrasting threads.

For the best looking cushions, match up the ribbons with the same type of fabric for the border surround and cushion back; team velvet ribbons with velvet, or satin ribbons with a shiny satin cushion.

For a standard 56cm (22in) square cushion pad you need about 60cm (¾yd) furnishing fabric, a 40cm (15¾in) square finished size woven ribbon panel, a 50cm (20in) square of iron-on interfacing and a 42cm (16½in) zip. For ribbon amounts see *Measuring for ribbon* below.

For more details on ribbons see pages 103–106.

▶ *Framing your woven ribbon panel with a toning fabric border not only highlights it, but also means you can enlarge it to make a cushion cover of whatever size you desire.*

**Measuring for ribbon** Measure and note the widths of your chosen ribbons. Decide on the panel size required and draw the shape on to paper. Use a ruler and pencil to draw a plan of the warp (vertical) ribbons, adjusting the panel shape slightly to accommodate the different ribbon widths or colour sequence as necessary. Colour in the design. Then draw another identical panel shape and mark and colour in the weft (crossways) ribbons in the same way. To estimate the ribbon amounts, measure each line and add a bit extra to each one to allow for ease and seams.

**1 Preparing the warp** Mark the panel size on to the non-adhesive side of the interfacing. Add 1.2cm (½in) all round for seams and cut out. With the adhesive side up, pin the interfacing on to the board. Cut the ribbons for the warp to size, including seam and ease allowances. Following your plan and starting in line with one marked edge, pin the ribbons in place angling the pins outwards.

**2 Preparing the weft** Cut the weft ribbons to size. Following your plan and starting at one top corner, align the long edge of the first ribbon with the marked panel edge, and the cut ribbon edge with the interfacing side edge. Anchor with an angled pin. Lay the next ribbon next to this and pin. Position a few more ribbons in this way.

**4 Bonding the ribbons** Using a cool setting on the iron and a pressing cloth, press between the angled pins to fix the ribbons to the interfacing. Carefully remove the pins. Turn over the work and press the back with a steam iron, or use a damp cloth and a hot iron. Leave to cool.

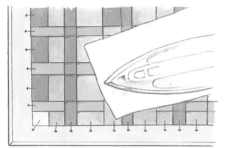

**6 Completing the border** Cut two more fabric strips to the same width as the previous strips, and long enough to reach across the panel and two side borders. Mark the seam allowance as before. With right sides of fabric together, pin then machine stitch the strips in place, stitching along the marked lines. Press the seams open.

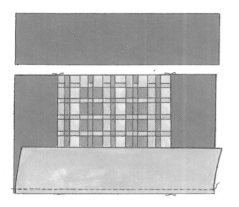

**3 Weaving** Fasten a safety pin to the free end of the first weft ribbon. With the ribbon side in line with the panel outline, pass the ribbon *over* the first warp ribbon. Weave the ribbon under and over across the warp to the other side. Pin the end to secure. Transfer the safety pin to the second weft ribbon. Weave by taking the ribbon *under* the first warp thread. Repeat the sequence, pushing up the weft ribbons each time. Weave down to the marked panel base. Secure the ribbon ends with pins.

**5 Adding border strips** To make the cushion border, cut two fabric strips to the required border width, adding an extra 1.2cm (½in) to each side for seams, and to the same length as the warp ribbons. Mark the seam allowance on the wrong side of the fabric. With the right sides of the fabric together, pin a border strip to opposite sides of the panel in the direction of the warp ribbons, through the marked border and panel outlines. Machine stitch in place, taking care to avoid catching the ribbon selvedges. Press the seams open.

**7 Making up the cushion cover** Make up the cushion back, inserting the zip, and stitch it to the cushion front, following the instructions given in step 7, page 23.

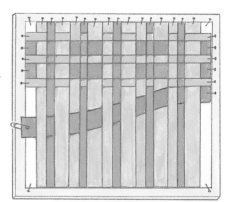

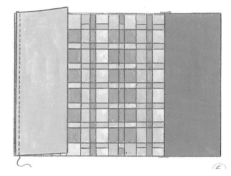

# WEAVING VARIATIONS

Try out different weaving techniques to create interesting three-dimensional effects, like the patchwork and zigzag weaves shown here. These patterns are quite simple to work – they owe their impressive looks to a careful choice of ribbon colours.

## PATCHWORK SQUARES

This weave creates a pattern of squares so it is important to work with equal width ribbons. The pattern uses three colours (**a**, **b**, **c**), with **a** as a pale shade and **c** as a dominant shade. Balance the finished weave sequence so that **c** has an **a**, **b**, **a** sequence on each side of the panel.

**1** **Preparing the warp** Pin an odd number of ribbons side by side in sequence **a**, **b**, **a**, **c**; **a**, **b**, **a**, **c**, and so on across the backing.

**2** **Weaving the pattern** Following the same colour sequence, weave ribbons **a**, **b**, **a**, **c** across the warp in the following way:
*First row* Weave ribbon **a** under one ribbon, then in sequence over two, under two, over two, under two to the end.
*Second row* Weave ribbon **b** under one ribbon, over one, under one, over one to the end.
*Third row* Weave ribbon **a** over two ribbons, under two, over two, under two to the end.
*Fourth row* Weave ribbon **c** over one ribbon, then in sequence under one, over three, under one, over three to the end.

## ZIGZAG WEAVE

This design can be worked with ribbons **a**, **b** of equal or different widths in two colours.

**1** **Preparing the warp** Pin an odd number of warp ribbons on to the backing fabric, alternating colours **a** and **b**.

**2** **Weaving the zigzags** Alternate colours **a** and **b** as follows:
*First row* Weave ribbon **a** over two ribbons, under two, over two, under two to the end.
*Second row* Weave ribbon **b** under one ribbon then in sequence over two, under two, over two to the end.
*Third row* Weave ribbon **a** under two ribbons, over two, under two, over two to the end.
*Fourth row* Weave ribbon **b** over one, then in sequence under two, over two, under two to end.

▶ *Decorative jacquard ribbon woven across a background of shimmery satin ribbons creates a new twist for a simple basket weave design. To create the effect, work a basic weave in two balanced colours, like the red and blue here, then weave in a narrower decorative ribbon across alternate rows of the weft, or vertically on the warp.*

patchwork s

zigzag w

basket w

# TAILORED BOLSTER COVERS

*For sleek lines and sharp tailoring, a smoothly covered bolster cushion is hard to beat and adds instant sophistication to a sofa or day bed. By following a few simple guidelines you can achieve flawless results.*

**N**estling by the arms of a sofa, propping up the pillows on a bed or perched elegantly at the head of a chaise longue, bolster cushions are elegant accessories, whose slender, elongated shape flatters most styles of furniture. You can cover them in a number of ways, ruching or pleating the ends and finishing them with a bright button or silky tassel; but for the ultimate in understated chic, a smoothly fitted cover with crisply piped edges is hard to beat.

Achieving a neat, well fitted finish is the key to success with this style of cover. Measure up and cut out the fabric carefully, and follow the stitching instructions overleaf to achieve perfect curving seams at each end of the cushion. The cover has a long zip opening so you can easily slip it off for cleaning when necessary.

Make the cover in any furnishing fabric of your choice. You can buy bolster pads in a range of standard sizes or have them made to order.

*Fabrics of all kinds suit the simple lines of a fitted bolster cushion cover. You can use a small or medium-scale all-over design, like this fresh blue and white woven check, or opt for one with a large repeating motif, which you can centre on the ends of the cushion.*

# MAKING A TAILORED BOLSTER COVER

These instructions show how to make a smooth, flat-ended bolster cover with a piped trim. Make sure you position the fabric attractively on the end pieces for the best results.

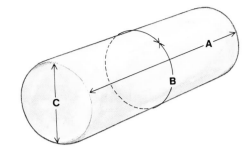

**1 Cutting out the body** Measure the length (**A**) and the circumference (**B**) of the bolster pad and add 3cm (1¼in) to each measurement for seam allowances. Cut a rectangle of fabric to this size.

**2 Cutting out the ends** Measure the diameter of one end of the bolster pad (**C**), add 3cm (1¼in) then divide by two. Set the compass to this measurement and use it to draw a circle on to paper. Cut out the circle and use it as a pattern to cut two circles from fabric, centring motifs.

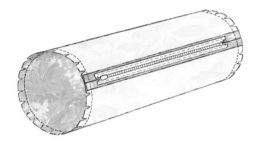

**3 Stitching the body** With right sides facing, fold the body in half lengthways and tack along the long edge. Measure and mark the position of the zip centrally along the seam. Machine stitch up to the marks at each end. Press open the seam and position the zip face-down over it. Tack and stitch the zip in place down each side and across the ends. Staystitch around each end of the body, 12mm (½in) from the raw edge. Snip to the staystitching at intervals. Remove the tacking stitches. Open the zip.

**4 Piping the end pieces** Make up two lengths of covered piping, each long enough to fit around the circular end pieces plus 4cm (1½in). With right sides together and using the machine zip foot, pin and stitch the piping in place around the edge of each end piece, snipping into the piping seam allowances for ease and neatly butt-joining the ends.

**5 Making up** With right sides facing, tack one end piece to one end of the body, spreading the clipped seam allowances so the seamlines can be matched. Repeat to attach the other end piece. With the body uppermost, stitch the ends in place using the zip foot. Remove the tacking stitches and clip into the end pieces so the seams will lie flat.

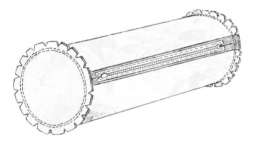

**6 Finishing the cover** Trim the seams if necessary. Turn the cover right side out via the zip opening. For a defined shape, use a knitting needle to gently push out the seamlines at each end.

◪ *The wide stripes on the bolster cover to the left are carefully positioned on the end pieces to lie perfectly symmetrically. The bolster on the right has a less tailored, quick-sew cover made from a single tube of fabric, pleated into the centre at each end and finished with a tassel.*

# FABRIC-COVERED LAMPSHADES

*These stylish no-sew lampshades can be made at very little cost and in next to no time – all you need is a piece of fabric that coordinates with your room scheme.*

Next time you make curtains or have your sofa re-upholstered, buy a little extra fabric to cover a lampshade; or any fabric remnant can be used. The slope of the lampshade will dictate the amount of fabric needed, but a coolie shade with a 33cm (13in) diameter will require a piece approximately half a metre (half a yard) square. Drum lampshades will use less fabric than a similarly sized coolie shade. Trace the pattern on to newspaper first to work out amounts, before buying the fabric. Buy an inexpensive lampshade and a tube of all-purpose adhesive from a home improvement store and you are ready to go.

The most important part is cutting out the fabric to fit the lampshade exactly, with just enough fabric overlapping to glue down in a rolled edge finish. Wrap the fabric round the lampshade at each stage and make any necessary adjustments.

Once the shade has been covered you can add trimmings and other embellishments – braiding, beading, lace, ribbons or tassels – anything that catches your fancy can be used as a final decorative flourish.

*Choose a lampshade fabric that coordinates with your decor – for a fun finishing touch add a decorative trim to plainer fabric.*

# COVERING THE LAMPSHADE

**1 Making the pattern** Place shade, seam down, on newspaper and mark the top and base seam position. Starting from the seam and tracing around base with a soft pencil, gently roll the shade until you reach the seam again. Roll the shade back along the traced base line, this time tracing the top edge. Add a 2.5cm (1in) seam allowance to curved outer edges of the pattern and 1cm (⅜in) to straight ends. Cut out the pattern and use to work out the amount of fabric needed.

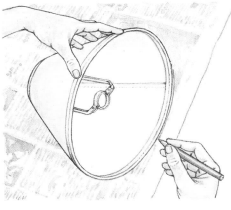

**5 Neatening the join** Apply a thin line of glue on top of the glued end and leave till tacky. Smooth down the turned edge to cover the raw end, then leave to dry.

**2 Checking the fit** Wrap the pattern around the lampshade to check the fit and make any adjustments that are necessary. There should be an overlap of 2cm (¾in) on the straight ends and an extra 2.5cm (1in) top and bottom.

**3 Cutting out the fabric** Position the pattern on the fabric so that any design on the fabric will be well displayed, and cut out fabric. Press under the 1cm (⅜in) seam on one straight end of the fabric to neaten.

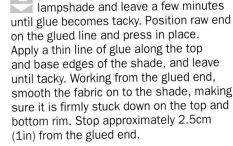

**4 Glueing the fabric** Put a thin line of glue along the seam of the lampshade and leave a few minutes until glue becomes tacky. Position raw end on the glued line and press in place. Apply a thin line of glue along the top and base edges of the shade, and leave until tacky. Working from the glued end, smooth the fabric on to the shade, making sure it is firmly stuck down on the top and bottom rim. Stop approximately 2.5cm (1in) from the glued end.

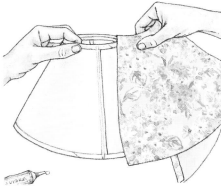

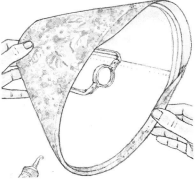

**6 Finishing the shade** If necessary, trim the top and base seam allowances. Apply glue sparingly to the wrong side of the seam allowance and leave until tacky. Fold the seams to the inside of the shade and press them down firmly. Leave to dry before glueing on any trimmings you are using.

▲ *Blue and gold fabric in an attractive design reminiscent of the Arts and Crafts era wraps a drum lampshade. A shiny brass stand echoes the gold in the fabric.*

▲ *An almost plain gold fabric is used to great effect on this coolie shade, with the rich colour emphasized by twisted braid in white, yellow and dark gold.*

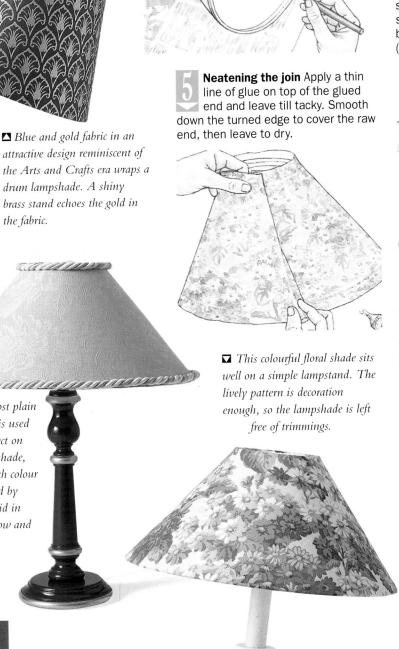

▼ *This colourful floral shade sits well on a simple lampstand. The lively pattern is decoration enough, so the lampshade is left free of trimmings.*

# FABRIC BED HANGINGS

*The bed is rightly the centre of attention in the bedroom, so don't leave the wall above the bedhead bare – crown it with an eye-catching fabric hanging for a simple but dramatic effect.*

W hatever the look and feel you desire for your bedroom – whether light and summery, soft and romantic, or rich and opulent – the right fabric hanging over the bedhead can help you achieve it.

Choose the fabric backdrop to fit in with the overall room style. For an understated, impressive finishing touch, hang a panel of exotic or exclusive fabric on the wall above the bedhead. Whether it be an antique piece of tapestry, an ethnic rug, a patchwork quilt or just a favourite bold-coloured blanket, centred over the bedhead it can have a dramatic impact, like that of a large painting.

Alternatively, drapes or curtains sweeping right down to the floor from well above the bedhead create an impression of comfort and height. And you don't have to go to the trouble and expense of a formal coronet or half-tester canopy. Simply hang the drapes from hooks or poles for a more casual but no less elegant result. For maximum impact the drapes should be as full and billowy as possible, and spill on to the floor in generous pools, so don't skimp on the fabric.

*Elegant lilies and a light, bright colour scheme give this bedroom a sunny, summery look – and pride of place goes to the fabric panel at the head of the bed. It forms a focal point in the room and is a cost effective way of introducing a more lavish fabric into a scheme.*

▶ **Display a precious rug** *safely out of harm's way on a wall. The texture and rich tones of this rug add extra warmth to the room and provide a change of pace to the other furnishing fabrics.*

▲ **This antique cotton quilt** *takes pride of place on the wall where it makes a lovely and unusual backdrop for the bed. A slim brass curtain pole, mounted on the wall, supports the quilt.*

◀ **A sweep of muslin**, *draped over wooden holdbacks, crowns the bed in this small room without being overpowering. Lightweight fabric wall-hung decorations give a small room a feeling of spaciousness.*

▶ **Folds of lace** *cascading down from a curtain pole, and caught in place with clusters of organza roses, make this bed the romantic centrepiece of the room.*

# BED HANGINGS

*Add presence and flair to an ordinary bed by crowning it
with a sweep of fabric, hung from two ceiling-mounted poles and
left to trail half or the whole way down to the floor.*

A sweep of fabric suspended from poles above a bed frames it beautifully, turning it into the focal point of a room and giving it the visual impact of a four-poster. Once you've located the ceiling joists, putting up the support poles is a straightforward task, and making up the fabric bed hanging is as easy as simply lining a length of fabric; or if you choose a cloth that looks good from both sides – a voile for example – hemming the ends is all that's required.

Choose fabric and fittings to suit the mood of your bedroom – a length of sprigged cotton hung from two pine poles for an airy country-cottage look, dreamy sheer fabric tied with ribbons to wrought iron rods for a romantic mood, or velvet drapes on gilt poles with ornate finials for a touch of opulence.

Look for fabrics to tone or contrast with your bedroom colour scheme and the rest of your soft furnishings. You can match the hanging to your curtains or bedlinen, or pick strong, contrasting colours so that the bed becomes the centre of attention. Low-cost fabrics such as cotton lining fabric, muslin, calico or even cotton/polyester sheeting are very effective, and make good economic sense as you need a fair amount of fabric for the drapes.

You can adapt the hanging in all manner of ways to create exactly the look you want – it can fall right to the floor or stop partway down, hang fairly straight or in a generous curve, lie flat or gathered, and have straight or shaped ends. You can add extra style with a contrasting lining, a decorative border or a pretty edging trim.

*A floral-print fabric panel, hanging in a gentle curve over the bed, is extended to create a sleek wall panel which also serves as an improvised bedhead.*

# MAKING A BED HANGING

### YOU WILL NEED

❖ STEPLADDER

❖ FOUR LARGE SCREW EYES and ROPE or CURTAIN POLE FIXTURES

❖ TWO POLES, CURTAIN or IMPROVISED

❖ BALL OF STRING

❖ MASKING TAPE

❖ TAPE MEASURE

❖ MAIN FABRIC

❖ LINING FABRIC

❖ MATCHING THREAD

❖ SCISSORS

❖ TAILORS' CHALK

The instructions given here show how to make a *lined ungathered hanging* suspended from the ceiling on wooden poles. If you're not sure about the length, drape an old curtain or sheet over the poles so that you can stand back and study various effects. This hanging is held in place on the poles with casings stitched across the fabric width.

If you want to make an *unlined gathered hanging*, choose a fabric that looks good from both sides. Calculate the hanging width by multiplying the desired finished width (usually the bed width) by 1½-2, depending on the fullness required. A casing can look bulky when gathered, so secure the gathered hanging to the poles with staples, tacks or drawing pins, or use spots of touch-and-close tape (Velcro).

## SUSPENDING THE HANGING

To suspend the hanging, you can use two standard curtain poles and fixtures attached to the ceiling, or, if the ceiling is very high or you want a hanging just above the bed, you can hang two poles on lengths of rope or cord fixed to the ceiling with large screw eyes. Thick wooden dowels, broom handles or sturdy bamboo canes could be used instead of curtain poles unless you are using proper curtain fixtures. The poles should be 20-30cm (8-12in) longer than the width of the bed. Be sure to screw the fixings into ceiling joists for a sound support – remember the bed hanging will be at least as heavy as a pair of curtains.

Another option is to suspend the bed hanging from fine brass wires extended across the ceiling – see overleaf for details.

**1 Hanging the poles** Locate the most suitable ceiling joists over the bed.
*Using rope* Screw the four screw eyes in place in pairs into the ceiling joists. Cut the rope into four equal lengths and tie one end of each length securely to a screw eye, and the other ends in pairs to the two poles so they hang straight and at the same height.
*Using curtain pole fixtures* Attach the curtain pole fixtures securely to the joists and fit the poles in place in the usual way.

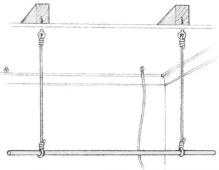

**2 Measuring up** Starting at the bedhead end, run the string from the desired drop to the first pole and tape in place; take the string across to the second pole, allowing a slight swag, and tape in place, then drop it to the required length at the foot of the bed and cut off the excess. Mark the position of the casings where the string crosses the poles. Untape the string and measure it to find the length of the finished hanging. The width is the same as the bed width.

**3 Cutting out** Cut out one rectangle of main fabric and one of lining fabric to the required size, adding 3cm (1¼in) to the width and length for seam allowances.

**4 Marking the casings** To find the casing width, measure round one pole. Place main fabric and lining right sides together, with raw edges matching. Pin and tack together. Using the marked piece of string as a positioning guide, mark with tailors' chalk the positions of the two pole casings on the fabric side

◀ *A bed hanging can be as long as you like – this one sweeps the floor at the foot of the bed. The lined length of fabric is gathered over two wooden dowels – it's a good idea to tether drapes hung in this way to the poles with pieces of touch-and-close tape (Velcro) to stop them sliding off.*

◀ *If you want to match your bed hanging to your curtains, you can go one better and suspend it from matching curtain poles – particularly if the poles are as attractive as these. The fabric used for the border on the bed hanging makes a neat reappearance on the curtain valance.*

## ADDING A BORDER

**1** **Cutting out** To add a contrasting border to the ends of your hanging, as shown in the picture opposite, first decide on the depth of the border. Cut out four pieces of contrast fabric to this size by the width of the hanging, adding an extra 3cm (1¼in) to both measurements for seam allowances. Cut out the main fabric and lining as in step 3, *Making a Bed Hanging,* but subtract the depth of the two borders from the length.

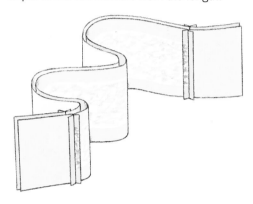

**5** **Stitching the hanging** Taking 1.5cm (⅝in) seam allowances, machine stitch around all the edges, leaving gaps for the casings at the marked positions and a 40cm (16in) opening in one side edge for turning through. Clip corners.

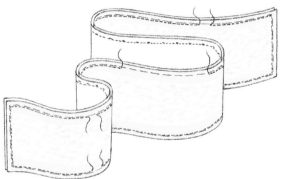

**2** **Stitching the border** With right sides together and raw edges matching, pin, tack and sew one border strip to each end of the main fabric and the lining pieces, taking a 1.5cm (⅝in) seam allowance. Press the seams open. Then follow steps 4-7, *Making a Bed Hanging.*

**6** **Stitching the casings** Remove the tacking, turn the hanging right side out and press. Slipstitch the large opening closed. Pin, then lightly mark out the casing positions across the width of the hanging. Machine stitch along these lines. Turn under the raw edges at the casing openings and slipstitch in place.

**7** **Finishing off** Take down the poles and slip one into each casing. Fix the poles back in place, making sure they are perfectly secure.

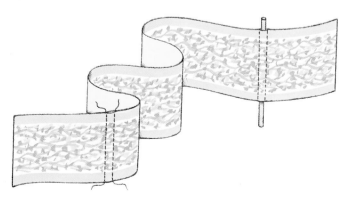

## LOCATING CEILING JOISTS

To find ceiling joists – usually spaced about 35-40cm (14-16in) apart – you can do one of the following:

❖

Tap across your bedroom ceiling – the tapping will sound hollow on plasterboard, and deeper when you reach a joist. When you think you have found a joist, poke the ceiling gently with a bradawl – it will sink straight through plaster and meet resistance at a joist.

❖

Lift up some floorboards in the room above so you can see the joists running at right angles underneath them. Tap the joists above the bed and ask a helper to mark their positions on the ceiling below. If your bedroom is on the top floor, look for the joists in the loft.

❖

Use a joist and batten detector. This is a small electronic meter which senses the change in density caused by a timber joist behind plasterboard.

❖

# WIRED BED HANGING

This multi-swagged hanging is held on four fine brass wires stretched across the ceiling over the bed. One wire runs just above the bedhead, another across the foot of the bed and the remaining two are equally spaced between. The wires are held in position by hooks on two opposite walls, and each piece of wire is fixed at one end to a cable tensioner – a threaded screw normally used for tightening up the support wires on electric cabling. You can buy cable tensioners from large home improvement shops. The fabric hanging is made up in the same way as those on the previous pages.

## YOU WILL NEED

❖ STEPLADDER

❖ STEEL TAPE MEASURE

❖ BRASS WIRE and WIRE CUTTERS

❖ EIGHT SCREW HOOKS

❖ DRILL and MASONRY BIT

❖ WALLPLUGS

❖ FOUR CABLE TENSIONERS and CABLE CLAMPS

❖ BALL OF STRING

❖ MAIN and LINING FABRIC

❖ MATCHING THREAD and NEEDLE

❖ SPANNER

**1 Measuring up** Measure from one wall across the ceiling to the opposite wall with a steel tape measure, adding 20cm (8in). Use wire cutters to cut four pieces of wire to this length.

**2 Screwing in hooks** Mark the wall positions for the hooks. Use a drill and masonry bit to make a small hole at each point, insert wallplugs and screw in hooks.

**3 Attaching the wires** Slip the end of a cable tensioner over a hook, and pass a length of wire through the other end; secure it with a cable clamp. Take wire across the ceiling, round the opposite hook and secure with a cable clamp.

**4 Making the hanging** Measure up with a ball of string, draping it from wire to wire in gentle curves. Cut out and stitch the bed hanging as for *Making a Bed Hanging*, but omit the casings.

**5 Hanging up** Starting at the bedhead, take the bed hanging up to the first wire and drape it over. Secure with a few stitches through the fabric layers just under the wire. Drape the hanging over the remaining wires.

◣ *A star-sprinkled midnight blue bed hanging, shaped into zigzags at one end and supported by taut wires, ripples across the ceiling.*

**6 Tightening the wires** Tighten the wires by twisting the middle section of the cable tensioner with a spanner, turning in one direction only. Twist in the opposite direction if you want to release the tension.

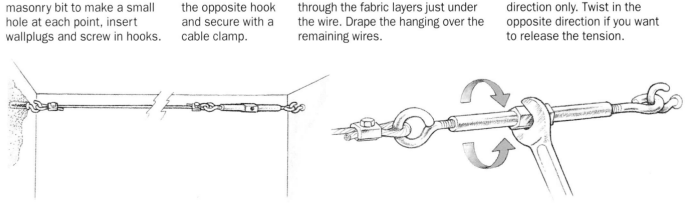

# MUSLIN BED DRAPES

*Give your bedroom a truly romantic look by swathing your bed in billowing clouds of sheer muslin. It's not expensive and you'll be delighted with the results.*

T he bedroom is the one room in the house where you can really create the scheme of your dreams. Only the chosen few see inside this room, so you can experiment to your heart's content and plan a fabulous boudoir fit for a princess. For a touch of fairy-tale escapism, try draping festoons of floating muslin or voile at the head of your bed.

You don't have to have a four-poster bed to achieve this look. An inexpensive canopy in a style reminiscent of old-fashioned mosquito nets works miracles fitted above a bed; you can buy these nets ready-made at little cost. You can, however, also make your own quick-and-easy version by hanging generous lengths of muslin – sufficient to envelope the entire bed – from a hook set in the ceiling.

If muslin draping all round the sides of a bed seems rather too confining, there is a visually pleasing alternative. Try draping swags of soft fabric around a square or circular framework mounted over the bed at ceiling height.

Fabric choices are not strictly limited to plain white – an array of patterned possibilities is readily available from most major department stores. Delicate sprigged patterns are ideal as a complement to a purely feminine bedroom, while muslin depicting celestially inspired patterns of stars, suns and moons makes a strong design statement. If you are feeling really adventurous, try dying the fabric to a soft all-over shade of pink or peach, or you could tie-dye it for a dreamy, cobweb-like effect.

*Sheer drapes dress a four-poster bed dramatically while retaining an airy look. Here the drapes hang from loops of sheer fabric, stitched across the top edge. Generous bows catch the drapes to each pole of the bed.*

◀ *It's hard to believe* that simple metal scaffolding, fixed out from the wall behind the bed, forms the support for these cloud-like festoons of muslin. The muslin is looped loosely in place so that it hides any evidence of the scaffolding.

▼ *Paisley-patterned* voile curtains, draped over a white pole set at the head of a bed, create a floating, romantic look. A pale peppermint green bow adds a purely decorative final touch on the end of the pole.

◀ *Children will love playing under* this dotted voile canopy, suspended over a spacious day bed. Net canopies similar to this are sold ready made.

# MOSQUITO NET CANOPIES

*Light and airy sheer fabric arranged into a softly draped canopy around the bed creates an enveloping cocoon that will appeal to the romantic in you.*

**M**osquito nets have their origins in hot, humid climes, where they're one of life's essentials for keeping bugs at bay while sleeping. Used in your own bedroom, they're more likely to fulfil a design rather than a practical role, transforming your bed into an escapist fantasy.

You can buy mosquito net canopies in kit form from some department stores and specialist stockists, or make your own. The kits are easy to assemble, but limit your design options – though you can customize them using trimmings, such as ribbons or appliqué motifs. Making your own net canopy is a simple task, and gives you great freedom of fabric choice – from straightforward muslin and sheers

woven with flecks or checks or stamped with individual, distinctive motifs, to intricately patterned lace designed to coordinate with your bedspread or curtain fabric, and even exotic jewel-coloured sheers shot with gold in the fashion of Indian saris.

The mosquito net canopy is supported by a hoop at the top, which helps it maintain its tented shape. If making your own canopy, you can use a large metal lampshade ring, a coolie lampshade frame, an old quilting hoop, or even a young child's plastic hula hoop for this purpose – a scout around the house will probably yield something suitable. Paint the ring or hoop white or an alternative shade to complement the canopy, or bind it with tape or ribbon.

*An ordinary divan bed is made into a focal point with the addition of a mosquito net canopy made from a fine white sheer. The simplicity of the canopy is perfectly in keeping with the room's fresh, pared-down blue and white scheme.*

# MAKING A MOSQUITO NET CANOPY

This canopy is created from six lengths of white muslin, stitched together and caught to the supporting hoop with ribbon ties. The canopy is suspended from a ceiling hook by means of a twisted cord and bead, so you can easily adjust the height if desired. Make the canopy at least long enough to touch the floor around the bed, and preferably a bit longer so it falls in rippling folds at the base. The canopy's finished width depends on the width of your sheer fabric – choose a wide fabric if you want a wide canopy.

## HANGING THE CANOPY

When deciding on the best position for the canopy, bear in mind the height of the ceiling. The canopy hoop is generally hung about 2.1m (7ft) from the floor, but you may need to experiment a little to achieve a good proportion. If you are unsure, hold the hoop temporarily in position with sewing thread or string and adjust until you are happy with the height.

Be sure to screw the hook supporting the canopy into a ceiling joist for a firm fixing.

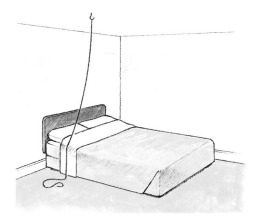

▶ *Stitched from finest muslin, a mosquito net canopy adds impact to the bed, yet doesn't take up much visual space because of the fabric's translucent nature. This makes it an excellent choice for small bedrooms, or rooms in which you want to maintain an airy ambience.*

**1** **Positioning the canopy** Decide on the best position for the canopy – usually centred over the bedhead, or above the middle of the bed. Check the ceiling for a joist at this point, and fix the hook in place; you may need to move the bed slightly to allow for the joist position.

**2** **Measuring for length** Tie one end of the string to the hook and take it out over the bed edges, down to the floor. Cut the string at the desired length, then take it down and measure it. Deduct the drop from the ceiling hook to where the top of the fabric canopy will lie (if any), and add 3cm (1¼in) for hems. Cut six fabric widths to this length.

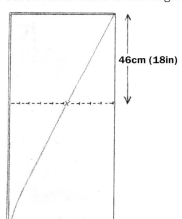

46cm (18in)

**3** **Shaping the top edges** Fold one fabric width in half. Measure 46cm (18in) down from the top of the folded edge and mark across the fabric width at this level with pins. Measure the circumference of the hoop and divide into 12. Measure this length along the pinned line from the fold, and mark lightly with a dressmakers' pencil. Use the pencil to draw a line from this point up to the top folded edge. Below the pinned line, graduate the line out to the full fabric width. Cut out 1.5cm (⅝in) beyond this marked line. Remove the pins and unfold the fabric. Repeat for each width.

**4** **Adding ribbon ties** Pin three fabric widths together down the side edges. Cut four 60cm (24in) lengths of ribbon. Fold two lengths of ribbon in half and slot the folded edge of each one between two fabric widths at the marked point, so they will hang on the *wrong side* of the canopy when the seams are stitched.

**5** **Seaming fabric widths** Using flat fell or French seams, stitch the pinned widths together, catching in the ribbon ties. Repeat steps 4 and 5 to make up the second half of the canopy.

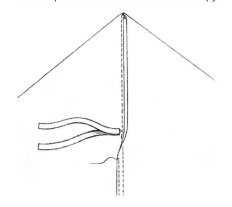

**6** **Creating the canopy** Pin and stitch together the two halves of the canopy down the centre back (omit the tie in this seam). Turn under a narrow double hem down each front edge to neaten; pin and machine stitch in place. Overlap the hemmed front edges, and pin and stitch through all layers from the top for 70cm (28in).

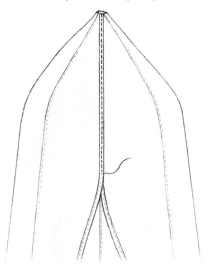

**7** **Finishing the edges** Neaten the base edge by turning under a double 1cm (⅜in) hem. Pin and stitch in place. Turn under the top edges and neaten, leaving a small hole for the cord to pass through.

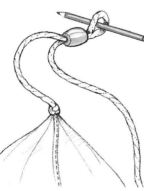

**8** **Adding the cord** Knot the twisted cord at one end and pull it through the opening in the top of the canopy, from the inside out. Knot again just above the fabric edge. If the bottom knot slips through, secure it with a few stitches. Thread the cord through the craft bead, then back again, slipping a pencil in the loop of cord if necessary to stop it slipping back through the bead.

**9** **Hanging the canopy** Insert the hoop in the canopy and secure with the ribbon ties. Hang the canopy in place by slipping the loop of cord at the end of the bead over the ceiling hook. Adjust until you are happy with the canopy height, then trim the cord to the desired length and knot the end, tying on a tassel for decoration if desired. Check the hoop lies perfectly level and adjust the ribbon ties if necessary.

# BUTTERFLY NET

If you like the idea of using a kit mosquito net canopy, but want to put your own design stamp on it, there are many options to choose from – including covering it with a scattering of fabric and net butterflies to create the dreamy effect shown here. See *Customizing Kits* below for other ideas.

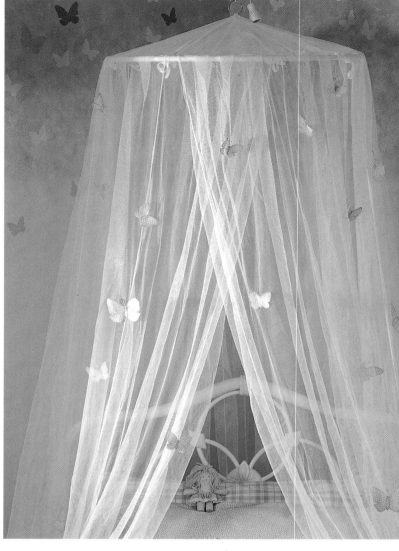

## YOU WILL NEED

- ❖ MOSQUITO NET KIT
- ❖ TRACING PAPER AND PENCIL
- ❖ STIFF CARD
- ❖ SCISSORS
- ❖ FUSIBLE WEBBING (BONDAWEB)
- ❖ FABRIC for butterflies
- ❖ CRAFT FLOWER-MAKING STAMENS for antennae
- ❖ NYLON NET
- ❖ MATCHING SEWING THREAD
- ❖ SILVER MACHINE EMBROIDERY THREAD

*Simple additions, like these fluttering butterflies made from a pink and white mini-print fabric and stiff pink nylon net, transform a plain kit canopy into a designer original.*

**1 Transferring the motifs** Trace the large and the small butterfly templates on to stiff card and cut out. Decide how many large and small butterflies you want. Draw around the templates *twice* for each butterfly on to the paper side of the Bondaweb. Cut out the butterflies and iron them on to the wrong side of the fabric. Cut out.

**2 Forming the butterflies** Remove the paper backing from the butterflies and iron them together in pairs, sandwiching a folded flower stamen between each pair at the head end of the body for antennae. For each fabric butterfly, cut two from net to the same size.

**3 Finishing off** Wind your sewing machine bobbin with thread to match the butterfly fabric, and use the metallic thread as the top thread. Using a narrow, close zigzag, stitch around the wings of each fabric butterfly, close to the edge. Lay two net butterflies over the top of each fabric one. Zigzag stitch the body outline through all the layers. Secure the butterflies to the mosquito net canopy with a few stitches through the body.

## CUSTOMIZING KITS

Bind the opening edges of the canopy with satin bias binding, in a pastel shade or a stronger colour to link it to other furnishings in the room.

❖

Make a pelmet of coloured sheer fabric to hang over the top of the existing canopy, creating a layered tent-like effect. Shape it to fit the ring as shown on the previous page, with a scalloped, zigzagged or tassel-trimmed lower edge.

❖

Handsew tiny glittery beads or dainty mother-of-pearl buttons at random all over the mosquito net for small twinkling details.

# PADDED HEADBOARDS

*A padded headboard adds the final touch of luxurious elegance to any bedroom. It protects the wall, makes the bed look more inviting and relaxing, and provides a soft backrest for sitting up in bed.*

U pholstered, foam-padded headboards are one of the most comfortable bed-head options for a divan bed. To finish the headboard you can add sumptuous detailing, like deep-buttoning, contrast piping or a ruched, complementary fabric border, as shown above.

The headboard is created by covering a board with a layer of thick foam. Then you add the main fabric for the centre panel, then the piping and finally the ruched border. All of these are fixed permanently to the headboard with adhesive and staples. The only sewing involved is in making the piping and gathering up the border fabric to form the ruched effect.

You can use most mediumweight furnishing fabrics for the headboard. As you have no way of cleaning the fabric once it is fixed in place, choose a fabric which is stain-protected, or treat the fabric with spray-on fabric protector before making it up. Bear in mind that a patterned fabric is less likely to show marks than a plain one.

The instructions overleaf are for re-covering a tatty old headboard, or for padding and covering a ready-cut headboard or a piece of plywood you cut out yourself. If you are re-covering a headboard, keep the old fabric pieces and use them as pattern pieces if they are still intact.

*A softly arched headboard looks graceful and is easier to cover than more complex bedhead shapes. An attractive combination of a floral border and plain blue centrepiece coordinates well with the bedspread and scatter cushions.*

# MAKING THE HEADBOARD

The instructions below include steps for making a shaped headboard from plywood. If you want to avoid cutting wood, use a ready-cut headboard base or make a rectangular headboard.

A headboard is usually 50-60cm (20-24in) high, measured from the top of the mattress (**A**). For the width, measure the bed width and add 7.5cm (3in) on each side (**B**) to allow for bedding.

You need one specialist material, called backtacking strip. This is a narrow strip of thin cardboard used to form a firm base for stapling the fabric, border and piping on to. It is available from upholstery suppliers or you can ask a local upholsterer to sell you some.

The inner fabric, border and piping are all stapled to the board along the piping line. To keep this area neat, staple at regular intervals rather than placing staples side by side, so that you can stagger the staples for each layer. You can buy staple guns and staples from department stores and home improvement stores.

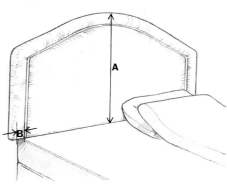

## PREPARING THE HEADBOARD

**1 Creating the design** Join pieces of paper together to make a sheet 15cm (6in) wider than the bed by 50-60cm (20-24in). Fold it in half widthways. Using the dinner plate or flexicurve, draw your chosen headboard shape on to the paper and cut it out. Open out the paper and pin it on to the wall at the head of the bed to check the size and shape, and adjust it if necessary. Mark the shape of the border – 10cm (4in) is a good width – by measuring at intervals in from the top and side edges and joining the dots to give a smooth, continuous line.

**2 Cutting the plywood and foam** Lay the pattern on the plywood and draw round it with a pencil. Clamp the plywood on a work bench and use a jigsaw or a panel saw to cut along the straight pencil line and a coping saw to cut round the curves. Lay one long edge of the foam level with the lower edge of the board and trim along the top and side edges so that the foam is 5cm (2in) larger than the board on these edges.

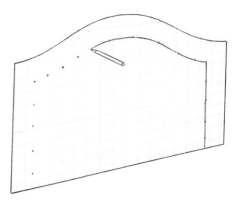

**3 Securing the foam** Apply adhesive to the face of the board and, with the bottom edge of the foam level with the board edge, stick the foam on top. Pull the excess foam around the sides and top of the board and staple it in place on the back with the staple gun.

**4 Marking the border** To transfer the inner line of the border on to the foam-covered board, cut off the border from the paper pattern to leave the inner section. With the lower edge level with the base, position this centrally on the foam and draw round it with a felt-tip pen.

**5 Stapling the backtacking strip** Lay the backtacking strip with one edge along the marked felt-tip line, cutting deeply into the edge to bend it around curves. Stapling along the centre of the strip, staple it through the foam to the board, spacing the staples 5cm (2in) apart. Use a hammer to tap in any stubborn staples. This strip creates a guideline and a firm base for stapling the centre fabric, ruched border and piping on to.

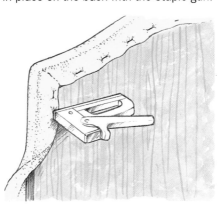

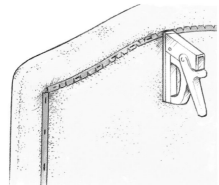

**5** **Gathering the border** Leaving 5cm (2in) ungathered at each end, work a long zigzag machine stitch over the narrow cord along one long edge of the long border strip of fabric, 6mm (¼in) in from the edge; alternatively, work rows of gathering stitches 6mm (¼in) and 12mm (½in) in from the edge.

**6** **Attaching the border** Fold the fabric strip into quarters and mark these sections on the gathered edge; divide the line of piping on the headboard into four also, and mark. Pull up the gathering on the fabric strip to fit the piped line. With right sides facing and raw edges matching, lay the gathered edge of the strip over the piping. Match the marks and staple. Adjust the gathers between the marks, leaving extra fullness at corners. Staple the rest of the strip in place, placing the staples closely together and stapling as close to the piping as you can. Staple the short ends to the back of the board.

# COVERING WITH FABRIC

**1** **Cutting the main fabric** For the inner section, cut the main fabric into a rectangle 4cm (1½in) larger in each direction than the area inside the backtacking strip. If you need to join two widths to make up the size, join two half widths on either side of a full width to avoid an unsightly central seam, taking care to match any pattern carefully. Press seams open.

**2** **Cutting the border and piping** For the ruched border, cut widths of fabric 15cm (6in) wider than the border, and join them to make a strip 2½-3 times longer than the top edge and two sides of the headboard. For the piping, cut sufficient strips of bias fabric to make a strip 5cm (2in) longer than the top and side edges of the inner section.

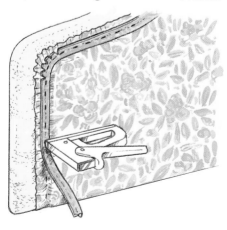

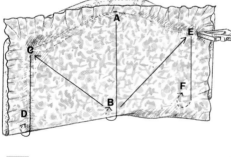

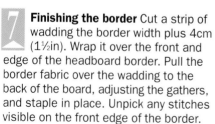

**3** **Covering the inner section** Lay the main fabric right side up over the front of the headboard, so that it extends beyond the backtacking strip by 4cm (1½in) all round. Avoiding the staples underneath, staple the fabric to the backtacking strip, first at the top (**A**), then at the centre lower edge on the back of the board (**B**). Put in a staple at one top corner (**C**) and at the bottom of the board on the back (**D**); repeat for the other side (**E**, **F**). Staple the fabric at 5cm (2in) intervals along the backtacking strip and at the back of the board. Trim the excess fabric to 1.5cm (⅝in).

**4** **Adding piping** Make up the piping. Taking the ends to the back of the board, lay the piping with the raw edges facing outwards and its stitching line over the staple line. Starting at the centre, staple along this line at 5cm (2in) intervals, clipping the piping for ease. Staple and trim the ends at the back.

**7** **Finishing the border** Cut a strip of wadding the border width plus 4cm (1½in). Wrap it over the front and edge of the headboard border. Pull the border fabric over the wadding to the back of the board, adjusting the gathers, and staple in place. Unpick any stitches visible on the front edge of the border.

**8** **Neatening the back** Use the headboard as a template to cut a piece of lining, and press under 12mm (½in) all round. Lay the lining on the back of the headboard to cover all the raw edges and staple in place.

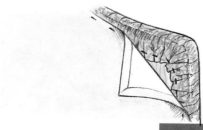

**47**

# FIXING THE HEADBOARD

For fixing headboards, most bed bases are fitted with two bolts at the head end. These are usually positioned about 15cm (6in) in from the sides, and about halfway down the base. You fix the headboard in place with two wooden battens, screwed into the back of the headboard and bolted to the bed base.

You can fix taller or heavier headboards which may have a tendency to wobble when secured to the base of the bed securely to the wall instead, with a pair of slot plates. These are two metal plates, one of which is screwed to the back of the headboard and the other to the wall. They slot firmly into one another so that the headboard sits tightly flush against the wall.

## FIXING WITH BATTENS

### YOU WILL NEED

- ❖ TWO WOODEN BATTENS 800 x 65 x 20mm (31½ x 2½ x ¾in)
- ❖ PENCIL
- ❖ DRILL AND WOOD TWIST BIT
- ❖ FOUR WOODSCREWS

**1 Drilling the bolt holes** Remove the bolts from the bed base. Stand one batten on the floor against the back of the bed base and mark the height of the bolt hole on the back of the leg. Repeat for the other batten. For each batten, drill a hole at the marked point large enough to take the bolt. Bolt the batten legs on to the bed.

**2 Positioning the headboard** Rest the headboard on the mattress against the battens and centre it. On the board mark the centre of each batten. On the battens, mark the corresponding central point and the mattress height. Unbolt the battens and drill two holes in each batten on the centre line, one 5cm (2in) up from the mattress mark and one 5cm (2in) down from the top of the batten. Lay the headboard face down on the floor and lay the battens on top, matching the marks. Screw the battens to the headboard. Bolt the battens on to the bed.

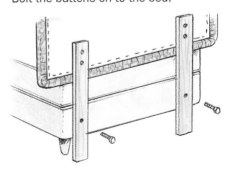

## FIXING WITH SLOT PLATES

*Padded headboards are great for children's rooms, giving a soft, comfy support which won't hurt if they bang their heads.*

### YOU WILL NEED

- ❖ TWO SETS OF SLOT PLATES
- ❖ DRILL AND DRILL BIT
- ❖ CAVITY FIXINGS OR WALLPLUGS
- ❖ SCREWS
- ❖ SCREWDRIVER

**1 Positioning the slot plates** Prop the headboard on the mattress and use a pencil to mark the centre top on the wall. Remove the headboard and position one half of each pair of slot plates with the tongues facing upwards, so they are on either side of the centre point of the board. Fix the slot plates to the wall.

**2 Fixing slot plates to the board** Before tightening the screws into the wall, leave them proud of the plates by 6mm (¼in) and put some chalk or ink on the heads of the screws. Offer the headboard up against the wall in the correct position and press against the screws to transfer the chalk or ink to the back of the headboard. Fix the other half of the plate facing downwards, at these marks, and drop the headboard on to the fixings.

# MACHINE-EMBROIDERED BEDLINEN

*Use your sewing machine to embroider decorative borders and motifs on to plain bedlinen. You can create all kinds of pleasing designs by simply adapting the basic machine stitches.*

**E**mbroidery on bedlinen gives it a special appeal, making it look just a little more luxurious than a simple printed design. Working your own machine-embroidered patterns and motifs on plain sheets and covers is surprisingly straightforward, as most modern sewing machines have a zigzag facility which allows you to work satin stitch. Even if your machine does not have the necessary swing arm, you can still embroider by making minor adjustments to the machine; you can use straight stitch and unusual threads to create linear designs that look just like corded embroidery.

If you are new to machine embroidery, the best approach is to aim for a clear,

graphic effect – with a good colour balance, simple designs can often look just as impressive as complicated professional embroidery. The designs on the following pages are an ideal starting point as they are based on straight lines, with no tricky shaping, and follow a clearly marked pattern. This means you can produce distinctive effects with basic sewing machine skills.

You can embroider ready-made bedlinen – simply unpick the side seams for access where necessary on pillowcases and duvet covers – or start from scratch by embroidering plain sheeting, ready for you to make up into covers. You can launder the embroidered bedlinen in the usual way.

*Creating a pattern of bold satin stitch stripes in zingy colours is a perfect introduction to machine embroidery. The contrast between the formal grouping of the border stripes and the randomly placed smaller blocks of motifs creates a lively graphic effect on this crisp white bedlinen.*

# WORKING MACHINE EMBROIDERY

Before starting on an embroidery project, it's a good idea to get re-acquainted with your sewing machine; make sure it is clean and well oiled, and check the handbook for different operating options. Fit a new, fairly fine needle suited to the fabric weight. Suitable sizes are generally 70-90 (9-14), depending on the thickness of the thread you are using. The designs featured here are worked using ordinary polyester or cotton-coated polyester sewing thread, but you can also use finer machine embroidery thread for working satin stitch.

The simplest way to work machine embroidery is by stitching along a pattern guideline, drawn on to the fabric with a dressmakers' marker pencil. For more complex designs you can first draw the pattern on to tissue paper, then tack it to the fabric and stitch over the drawn line; the paper falls away as the needle tears through it (see overleaf for this method).

To prevent the fabric puckering while working satin stitch, stabilize the stitching area with tear-off backing material – a paper-like product specially designed for decorative needlework (see *Striped Satin Stitch Bedlinen* below).

## DESIGN OPTIONS

Border and motif designs are a good combination for bedlinen because they are so versatile. You can work a border pattern along the top edge of a duvet cover, across the turn-back on a top sheet, all round the edges of a pillowcase and even along the base edge of a valance. You can add interest by creating a coordinating motif – an element from the border perhaps, as shown below – and repeating it at widely spaced intervals all over the bedlinen. Or, for simplicity, just use the border on duvet covers and sheets, and work a single corner motif on pillowcases.

The same design will look completely different depending on the colours chosen for the stitching. For a dramatic effect, choose a bold colour for the embroidery to contrast with the sheeting. To create a softer look, opt for embroidery in colours to tone with the sheeting. For a really subtle effect – and one that never dates – work the embroidery in a matching colour; white on white is a classic combination.

# STRIPED SATIN STITCH BEDLINEN

This simple three-stripe border design is repeated as random motifs all over the bedlinen. It's an easily adaptable design – just repeat the motif as many times as necessary to make up the required border length. You can also take the basic elements of the design and rearrange them to create a different effect – double up the border stripes to make a bold band right across the centre of a duvet cover, or alternate the direction of each three-stripe block to create a basketweave effect.

Experiment on a scrap of sheeting to see whether you can work a line of satin stitching in one go, or whether you need to work twice over the design line as shown in steps 4-5, to stop the fabric puckering up. This depends on your machine.

### YOU WILL NEED
- ❖ READY-MADE BEDLINEN OR SHEETING
- ❖ TRACING PAPER AND PENCIL
- ❖ CARDBOARD for templates
- ❖ CRAFT KNIFE AND CUTTING MAT
- ❖ DRESSMAKERS' PENCIL
- ❖ TAPE MEASURE
- ❖ TEAR-OFF BACKING (STITCH 'N' TEAR)
- ❖ SEWING MACHINE WITH ZIGZAG FOOT
- ❖ SEWING THREAD in three colours, and thread to match bedlinen

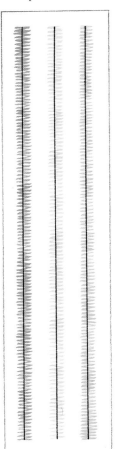

border stripe template

random motif template

**1** **Making templates** Trace the stripes on each template on to a piece of cardboard. Using a craft knife and mat, cut away a thin strip of card over each stripe, just wide enough for a pencil point to fit through. Unpick seams where necessary on duvet covers and pillowcases to allow access for stitching. Press the bedlinen.

**2** **Marking up the design** Starting at the centre, use a ruler, the *border stripe template* and a dressmakers' pencil to measure and mark three-stripe border blocks along the edge(s) of the bedlinen, lining them up with the seam stitchlines and spacing them about 2.5cm (1in) apart; you may need to adjust the spacing slightly so the motif fits evenly. Mark right to the stitchline at the end of the fabric if working a single border, or leave the corner free as shown if working the border all round. If desired, use the *random motif template* to mark motifs at intervals across the bedlinen.

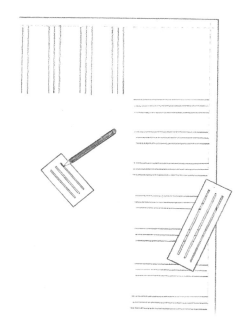

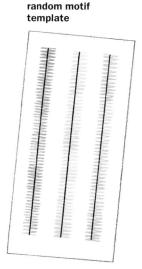

## EXPERIMENTING

To gain confidence in your machine embroidery skills, try working different zigzag and satin stitch effects on a spare piece of sheeting. Practise stitching varying the length and width of a stitch and using different threads. Practise stitching straight lines, working each line to show a change of width or stitch length. Try changing the stitch width gradually within a row to create wavy lines, or sharply to create arrowhead or diamond effects. Also, try creating pattern motifs by stitching short lines of satin stitch using different colours side by side or in a cross formation – you'll be surprised how quickly you can produce 'scribble' patterns this way.

▶ *Satin stitch stripes in purple, fuchsia and acid green give a crisp, modern feel to plain white bedlinen. Varying the thread colours gives this versatile design very different looks: try black thread for a minimalist Japanese style, a pastel mix for a softer look, or white on white for pure sophistication.*

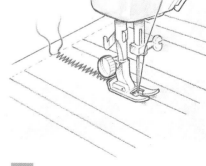

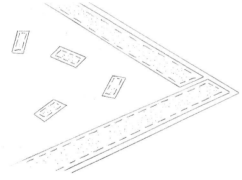

**3 Supporting the fabric** Pin and tack strips of tear-off backing to cover the area behind the marked border stripes, and pin and tack a piece behind each random motif.

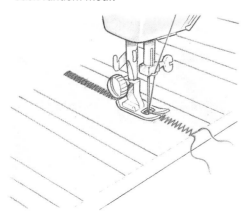

**4 Starting to stitch**
Thread the machine and bobbin with the first of the coloured threads. Set the machine to a fairly closed zigzag stitch and the stitch width to match the pattern. Starting on the border or random motifs, insert the needle to one side at the end of a marked stripe, and pull the bobbin thread through to the right side. Work a line of zigzag stitch down to the end of the marked stripe.

**5 Completing the first stripe** At the end of the stripe, pivot the needle and turn the work round. Close up the zigzag and stitch back down the line. To finish, pull the threads through to the right side and trim, leaving long ends. Secure these later.

**6 Working the stripe blocks** Stitch all the stripes in the first colour as described in steps 4-5. Re-thread the needle and bobbin with the second colour and work the second stripe in each block in the same way. Repeat to work the remaining stripes in the third colour.

**7 Finishing off** Carefully unpick the tacking stitches and remove the tear-off backing. Thread each thread end through a sewing needle, pull it to the wrong side and weave it into the back of the satin stitch to secure. Re-stitch any open seams on the bedlinen with matching sewing thread, and finally press it.

# CORDED BORDERS

This mock cording technique is worked with straight stitch – you don't need a sophisticated sewing machine. The linear design is stitched from the wrong side of the fabric, so the thicker decorative thread used in the bobbin becomes the top thread. As the decorative thread is hand-wound on to the bobbin, you can use threads such as button thread, cotton perlé and fine crochet threads which are too thick to machine stitch in the conventional way. You work the design through a clearly marked tissue paper pattern which tears away as you stitch.

This technique is suitable for any design with a long, continuous line, so it is ideal for creating repetitive patterns like this Greek key variation.

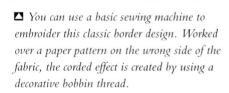

### 1 Preparing the machine
Thread the machine needle with polyester sewing thread. Hand-wind the decorative top-stitching thread evenly on to an empty bobbin and fit it into the machine. Allow sufficient to work the entire border without joins, if possible. For a large project, prepare two bobbins so you can carry on when the first runs out.

### 2 Checking the tension
Tighten the machine top thread tension slightly, and try out the stitching on a spare piece of sheeting to find the most suitable tension and stitch length. The normal sewing thread should pull slightly without puckering, so that the thicker bobbin thread, on the right side, lies almost flat on the surface of the fabric.

### 3 Making the pattern
Trace the border pattern given below on to a strip of tissue paper, and repeat on as many tissue strips as are needed to extend across the bedlinen.

## YOU WILL NEED
❖ BEDLINEN OR SHEETING
❖ MATCHING POLYESTER SEWING THREAD
❖ CONTRAST TOP-STITCHING THREAD
❖ SPARE PIECE OF SHEETING
❖ STRONG TISSUE PAPER
❖ PINS AND TACKING THREAD

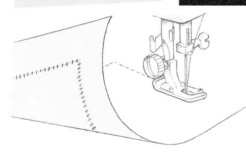

### 4 Working the design
Unpick seams where necessary on duvet covers and pillowcases to allow access for stitching. Press the bedlinen, then pin and tack the tissue patterns in place on the wrong side, overlapping the lengths and matching up the design lines. Carefully slip the work in place on the machine, positioning it to start sewing at one end of the border. Secure the threads with a back stitch, then stitch along the design lines to the end of the border. Secure as at the start.

▲ *You can use a basic sewing machine to embroider this classic border design. Worked over a paper pattern on the wrong side of the fabric, the corded effect is created by using a decorative bobbin thread.*

### 5 Finishing off
Remove the tacking stitches and any remaining pieces of tissue paper. Re-stitch any opened seams with matching thread, then press the bedlinen on both sides.

**Greek key border design**

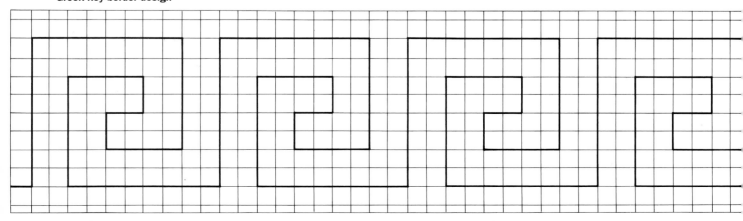

# INITIAL JOY

*Gently intertwining initials, spelling out your own or a loved one's name, make a distinctive decorative statement when they are used to embellish soft furnishings around your home.*

Personalize your home accessories and soft furnishings by embroidering or stencilling them with your initials. Elegant letters, intertwined to spell out the capitals of your own or your family's names, make an unusual and highly individual embellishment.

You can decorate all manner of home furnishings with a monogram – from the most discreet of scented sachets, to the upholstery on an easy chair. Use monograms to emblazon roller blinds, firescreens, table and bedlinen as your own personal heraldry.

Many embroidery books and pamphlets offer a tantalizing selection of beautifully drawn initials for you to copy. Hand embroidery – usually straightforward satin stitch – is the traditional way of adding your monogram on to fabric. You can use it to achieve delightfully subtle effects by embroidering in self-colour thread to match the item.

If you want instant results, stencilled monograms are another option and a twist on the traditional approach. Search out pre-cut stencils, or use books on calligraphy to devise your own interlocking initials. Stencilled in a slightly stronger shade than the background, or a bold contrast, the monograms make an exciting statement and an unusual alternative to printed fabric.

*Making monogrammed linen and handkerchiefs into exquisite bedding and home accessories preserves their beauty. You can find antique linen in second-hand shops and on market stalls – you can even use sections of damaged pieces.*

▲ **Stencilled monograms** *may well be the solution if embroidery is not your forté. The intricate interlocking initials on this upholstered footstool have immediate impact.*

◀ **Unusual jacquard table linen,** *woven with an all-over monogram design, becomes even more eyecatching when isolated letters are embroidered over in gold. Create a similar look by stitching initials on white damask or linen.*

▲ **The popularity of monograms** *means that you can find them on all sorts of decorative items. This pewter trinket box, and matching makeup mirror, would make a personal gift or ornament for a dressing table.*

▶ **Just three initials,** *centred on this chair cover, transport it from a pedestrian spare chair to a positively luxurious room accessory. Individual monograms like these are not time-consuming to embroider and are a suitable project for novice needleworkers. To continue the personalized touch, the monogram is also embroidered on to the blind behind the chair and the slippers.*

# ITALIAN QUILTED PILLOWS

*Create subtle three dimensional effects on pillow covers and bed cushions using decorative Italian quilting techniques. You can work these softly padded designs by hand or machine, as you choose.*

Quilted covers of all kinds have an enduring appeal and Italian quilting offers a versatile variation on the familiar theme, one you can use to complement any bedroom scheme. With Italian quilting only selected motifs are padded, so the results are decorative rather than insulating and, because the effects are quite subtle, the style blends well with other quilted or patterned fabrics. It is a perfect way to add textural interest to bed accessories such as cushion covers or removable day covers for pillows. You can choose to create designs with a linear, graphic quality or go for bolder padded effects.

There are two main styles of Italian quilting; corded and trapunto, and both are worked using a top fabric and a loose weave backing fabric such as muslin. The design outlines are machine or handstitched through both fabric layers, and the padding is inserted through small gaps made in the backing. These are then handsewn to secure and the back neatened with a lining fabric.

Italian corded quilting is made up of a series of quilted lines which are formed by parallel channels of stitching. You thread quilting wool or cotton cord through these channels to pad them and produce a raised outline.

Trapunto quilting has a puffy effect similar to regular quilting, but is more adaptable, as selected areas of a design can be exaggerated or minimized as desired with varying amounts of kapok or synthetic washable toy filling. For textural interest, you can incorporate both techniques together, and mount the finished work over polyester wadding for a further quilted effect.

*Italian corded quilting has a graphic quality, and this pretty hand-quilted cushion shows how elegant the technique can be. The motif can be adapted to make a decorative border for a bed cover or throw.*

# QUILTING WITH ITALIAN TECHNIQUES

The following instructions show how to work the bold trapunto quilting used to pad the letter motifs on the cushions pictured here, and the corded quilting technique used for the cushion on the previous page. As for all forms of quilting, the most suitable fabrics are natural, closely woven cottons, wool and silk. To machine stitch the design, use colour-matched topstitching thread for bold defini-tion, in a fibre to suit the fabric type. For hand quilted effects, use quilting thread, embroidery cotton or stranded thread. You can mount the work in a frame if desired.

Work the quilting before making up your cushion or pillow.

### TRANSFERRING DESIGNS

**For trapunto quilting** Before working a tra-punto design, draw your chosen motifs to actual size on paper and make a tracing for reference. Transfer the design to the muslin backing fabric, using either a light-coloured dressmakers' carbon paper or your preferred method, and remembering to reverse the motif as appropriate. Alternatively, you can use a soft pencil to transfer a freehand design on to the right side of the fabric.

**For corded quilting** Transfer the design to the backing fabric as for *trapunto quilting*. Each line of your design must consist of two parallel lines about 6mm (¼in) apart for your cord to sit between. Mirror image and geo-metric designs are particularly suited to this method as their linear qualities are enhanced.

# WORKING TRAPUNTO QUILTING

Tack the muslin backing, with the marked design right side up, to the wrong side of the fabric. If working by hand, you can mount the fabrics in a frame if desired.

To make trapunto cushion covers like those in the picture, you will need fabric for each one as follows: one 42 x 42cm (16½ x 16½in) square for the front from main fab-ric, muslin and lining, and two 42 x 30cm (16 x 12in) rectangles from main fabric for the back.

A trapunto design also adds a luxurious touch to a daytime cover for a pillow. You could complement the design by lining the pillowcase with lightweight wadding.

| YOU WILL NEED |
| --- |
| ❖ MAIN FABRIC |
| ❖ MUSLIN |
| ❖ LINING FABRIC |
| ❖ MATCHING SEWING THREADS |
| ❖ EMBROIDERY OR QUILTING THREADS (optional) |
| ❖ NEEDLE AND SMALL SHARP SCISSORS |
| ❖ TOY STUFFING OR KAPOK |
| ❖ TAPESTRY NEEDLE |
| ❖ CROCHET HOOK (optional) |

**1 Working the design** *By machine:* Select a medium length stitch and, with the marked design side up, work round the outline. Pull the thread ends to the muslin side and secure. *By hand:* With the marked design side up, use small running stitches or back stitch to work round the design outline.

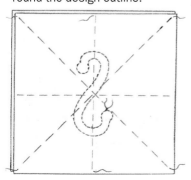

*Vibrant orange and yellow spell out a sunny message in any language. Making a series of cushions, each with its own padded letter motif, is an innovative way to use trapunto quilting.*

**2 Preparing for padding** When the design is complete, turn the work muslin side up. *For small shapes:* Use a tapestry needle to work a space between the muslin threads, ready for padding. *For larger shapes:* Cut a small slit in the muslin at the centre of each area to be padded, cutting on the straight grain if possible.

**3 Padding the motifs** Insert the padding material a little at a time, teasing it out carefully to avoid lumps. Use a crochet hook or tapestry needle to gently push the padding into place and distribute it evenly. Check the effect on the right side.

**4 Securing the padding** When each shape is padded, ease back the woven threads or bring the raw edges together with small overcast stitches. For a neat finish, pin and tack a piece of lining fabric over the muslin, and complete the sewing project using the three fabric layers as one.

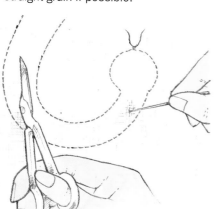

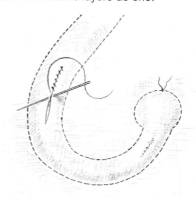

# WORKING CORDED QUILTING

Besides the materials listed for *Working Trapunto Quilting*, you will need quilting wool, available from specialist suppliers, or soft cotton cord or thick knitting yarn as a filling. Check that the yarn or cord chosen will fit through the narrow stitched channels of the design. If using cord, wash it to pre-shrink it before use. As the cord is threaded through the channels on a blunt needle, check that this can also fit through the stitched channels. As for trapunto, first tack the muslin backing, with the marked design right side up, to the wrong side of the main fabric.

**1** **Stitching the design** *By hand:* Fit the prepared main fabric and muslin in a frame and use a matching or contrast thread to stitch the design outlines. *By machine:* Stitch along the marked outline with small, straight stitches, working the design in a logical order, so the thread does not stop or start more than is necessary. Pull all the threads to the muslin side and secure them by tying them together in pairs.

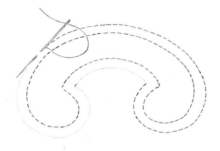

**2** **Inserting the cord** Thread a blunt-ended needle with filling cord. Try to gauge the correct length of cord for each channel. At the beginning make a small slit in the muslin backing, or use the needle to force the threads apart over a channel and thread the cord through the gap.

**3** **Padding the design** Run the needle along the channel for about 3cm (1¼in) and bring it out of the muslin. Re-insert it and repeat along the line in the same way.

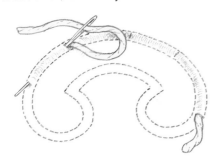

**4** **Shaping at angles and curves** Where the outline changes direction, bring the needle out of the muslin, re-insert it through the gap and pull it flat. Do not pull the cord too tight as this will pucker the fabric. At sharp angles, leave a small loop of cord outside the channel for ease. Leave a 3mm (⅛in) end at the beginning and end of each length of cord.

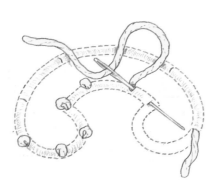

▲ *To make a corded quilting template, scale up this motif to your required size on a photocopier. Position the motif as on the cushion to form a quarter of the finished design, or place the motifs side-by-side to form a border.*

**5** **Finishing off** When the design is complete, turn to the right side to check the effect, and ease the padding as necessary. Pin and tack a piece of lining fabric over the muslin backing to neaten, and complete the sewing project using these three fabric layers as one.

# LACE-TRIMMED PILLOWCASES

*For sheer luxury with a classical simplicity and femininity,*
*pure white pillowcases, trimmed with lace and delicate hand-embroidery,*
*are the ultimate in romantic bedlinen.*

I t is possible to spend a fortune dressing a bed with frills and lace in a wonderfully self-indulgent, romantic fashion. However, by following a few practical shortcuts, you can create your own beautiful lacy designs with all the timeless appeal of exquisite heirloom linen, but for a fraction of the cost.

Start with a plain white pillowcase in good quality cotton or linen. You can either make your own or adopt the quick-and-easy approach and buy one. For attractive heirloom-type pillowcases, pure cotton, fine Egyptian cotton and linen fabrics look the most convincing. Then decorate the pillowcase front with a mixture of ready-made embroidered or lace-trimmed accessories, such as a table mat, traycloth, napkin or handkerchief. You can add

a frill round the edge of the pillowcase and disguise any fabric joins using strips of new or antique lace and ribbon.

Antique sales and bedlinen, fabric and tableware departments are good sources of accessories, trimmings and inspiration. You needn't worry about old lace being fragile; any delicate embroidery or antique linen is strengthened when mounted on the pillowcase.

Try, as far as possible, to match up the texture and whiteness of the different fabrics. If you can't match the lace trimmings exactly, select a toning cream or coffee-coloured lace, as the contrast adds definition to the design. Once you have trimmed the pillowcase, you can copy various elements from the design to trim a coordinating sheet or a duvet cover.

*Freshly laundered, this immaculate white lace-trimmed bedlinen looks fabulous set amidst the glowing colours of the richly patterned bolsters and drapes.*

# HEIRLOOM PILLOWCASE

These instructions are for making a pillow-case with a separate front panel and a back panel with flap opening. The front is decorated with a central panel made from a prettily embroidered, ready-made linen table mat. A border of strip lace, stitched with neatly folded mitred corners disguises the mat's edges. The outer lace border is inserted in the pillowcase seams.

If you prefer, you can start with a plain white ready-made pillowcase and unpick the seams to make a separate pillowcase front. Then you can add the embroidery or lace as if you are making your own pillowcase.

For the best results, first wash, lightly starch and iron all the fabrics before making the pillowcase.

**1 Cutting out the pillowcase** *For the front:* measure the pillow depth and add 3cm (1¼in) (**A**). Measure the length and add 3cm (1¼in) (**B**). Cut one rectangle of sheeting **A** by **B**. *For the back:* add 1.5cm (⅝in) to **B**, then cut one rectangle of sheeting to this new size by **A**. *For the opening flap:* cut one rectangle of sheeting **A** by 20cm (8in).

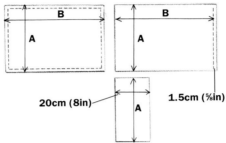

20cm (8in)     1.5cm (⅝in)

**2 Estimating for border lace** *For the mitred central panel border:* measure each side of the centre panel and add double the width of your chosen lace edging to each length. Finally, add 3cm (1¼in) for seams to the total length. *For the outer edge:* measure round the pillowcase edge and add 32cm (12½in) to allow 8cm (3¼in) for gently gathering the lace at each corner. Add 3cm (1¼in) for seams.

☑ *In close up, you can clearly see how the straightedge lace is zigzag stitched along both sides around the central panel and neatly mitred at the corner. The gathering of the border lace at the corner is also visible.*

**3 Preparing the centre panel** To mark the centre points, fold and press the pillowcase front and the central panel into quarters. With right sides up, place the panel over the pillowcase front with centres matching. Pin and tack to secure, then machine stitch close to the panel edge.

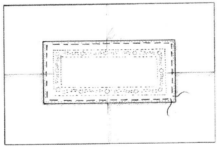

**4 Adding the inner lace border** Right side up, extend the straight-edge lace by a generous lace-width beyond the panel corner. With the inside edge of the lace strip covering the panel stitching line, pin and tack both edges of the strip to the fabric. At each corner, fold the lace to form a neat mitre. Tack along the mitre fold to secure.

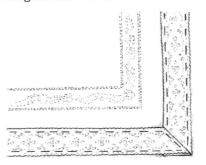

**5 Joining the border** At the cut ends, tuck the lace under so the folds align diagonally. Trim the excess to 1cm (⅜in) of the folds. Pin and tack to secure. Using a small, fairly open zigzag stitch, stitch along the mitre then along both straight edges of the lace and diagonally across the corners all round the panel. Remove tacking stitches.

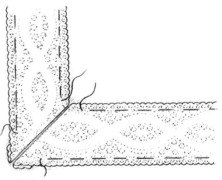

**6 Fitting the outer lace border** With a French seam, join the ends of the border lace to form a loop. Fold the lace loop in half and half again and mark the creases with pins. Fold the pillowcase in half lengthways and widthways and mark the creases. With the seam of the border loop slightly off centre, match the creases on the lace to the centre folds on the pillowcase. Pin and tack the lace smoothly around the edge to within 2cm (¾in) of each corner, leaving surplus lace free.

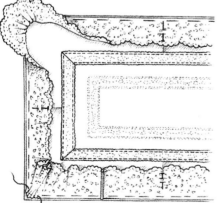

**Gathering the corners** Run a gathering thread through the free, excess lace at each corner and pull it up to fit. Pin and tack the lace in place round the corners and then machine stitch round the edge of the pillowcase front. Remove the tacking.

▲ *Despite its luxurious appearance, none of the fabrics used to make this romantic looking lace trimmed pillowcase are antique or exorbitantly expensive – which means you can create exquisite, heirloom-style bedlinen on a realistic budget. With its pretty lace trimmings, the basic pillowcase belies its humble origins – it is simply an inexpensive thick cotton pillow slip that is used as a pillow protector under a pillowcase. Its texture is an exact match to the central embroidered linen panel.*

**Assembling the pillowcase** Make up the pillowcase back and join it to the front piece. Turn right side out and press.

# T I P

**RIBBON-TRIMMED PANELS**
If you are decorating a pillowcase with an embroidered or lace panel which has an integral lacy border, attach the panel by stitching along the top of the lace so the lacy gathers fall freely. Cover the stitching line with a line of narrow ribbon, using a matching thread to topstitch along its selvedges.

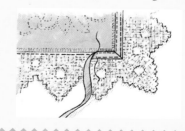

# SCENTED PILLOWCASE

You can complement romantic, lace-trimmed bedlinen by adding a pretty little scented pillow as a finishing touch. Make the pillowcase from linen or fine quality cotton sheeting, such as percale, and trim it with luxurious heavy cotton lace. The pillowcase here has a plain centre, but if you like, you could mount a piece of embroidered linen in the same way as described for the pillowcase on the previous page, or add a personal touch with an embroidered monogram.

You also need to make a pad to fit the pillowcase. For soothing aromatherapy, you can fill the pad with a mixture of soft cushion filling and pot pourri or a bouquet of herbs.

Fabric amounts are for a pillowcase with a finished size of 34 x 25cm (13½ x 10in). You can adapt these measurements for different sizes of scented pillows. The instructions include 1.5cm (⅝in) for seams.

## YOU WILL NEED

❖ 40cm (½yd) STRONG COTTON FABRIC for pad cover

❖ 40cm (½yd) FINE WHITE COTTON FABRIC

❖ 2.2m (2½yd) COTTON LACE, 6cm (2¼in) wide

❖ 1.2m (1⅜yd) SATIN RIBBON, 1cm (⅜in) wide

❖ DRESSMAKERS' PEN

❖ MATCHING SEWING THREADS

❖ 20cm (8in) ZIP

❖ TAPE MEASURE

❖ POTPOURRI

❖ POLYESTER FILLING

**1 Preparing the fabrics** *For the front:* cut a 37 x 28cm (14½ x 11in) rectangle from fine cotton or linen fabric. *For the back:* cut two 28 x 20cm (11 x 8in) rectangles from fine cotton fabric. *For the inner lace border:* match up the lace scallops and cut two 27cm (10¾in) strips and two 20cm (8in) lace strips. *For the outer lace border:* match up the lace scallops to meet at each corner and cut two 49cm (19¼in) strips and two 40cm (15¾in) lace strips. *For the pad cover:* cut two 36 x 27cm (14¼ x 10¾in) rectangles from strong cotton fabric.

**2 Creating the centre panel** Press the pillowcase front into quarters to find the centre. Use the dressmakers' pen to mark a 16 x 8cm (6¼ x 3¼in) rectangle centrally on the pillowcase front.

**3 Trimming the panel with lace** Pin, tack and stitch the lace level with the marked line, then follow *step 5, Heirloom pillowcase* on the previous page to mitre the corners. To hold the lace flat, work a further line of stitching 3cm (1¼in) outside the first stitching line. Remove the tacking stitches.

**4 Adding the ribbon trim** Starting at one corner, pin and tack the ribbon over the lace edge, folding the ribbon into a mitre at each corner. Machine stitch in place along each ribbon selvedge. Remove the tacking. Tie the remaining ribbon into a bow and trim the ribbon ends at an angle to prevent fraying. Position the bow over the ribbon join and machine stitch through the knot to secure.

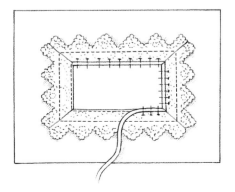

**5 Mitring the lace border** Lay the pillowcase front right side up. With edges level, pin the lace strips on the fabric to check the fit, then pin the corners diagonally to shape mitre joins. Remove the lace and stitch the mitres with a French seam. Re-position the lace on the fabric and machine stitch in place.

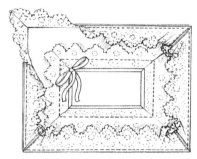

**6 Joining the back piece** Fit the zip centrally between the two back pieces. Open the zip slightly. Pin the lace to the pillowcase front to avoid catching it during stitching. With right sides together and, pinning through the lace border stitching line, pin, tack, and machine stitch the pillowcase back to the front.

**7 Making the pad** With right sides together and edges aligned, pin and tack the pad cover pieces together. Machine stitch round, leaving a gap in one side. Clip the corners and turn right side out. Pad the cover with a mixture of polyester filling and potpourri. Slipstitch the opening closed. Fit the pad in the zipped pillowcase.

☑ *A matching fragrant pillow is the perfect accessory for a bed styled with romantic white cotton lace. Scent the pillow with a favourite potpourri, or ensure restful nights with a filling of calming herbs.*

# LACY BEDROOMS

*Light and airy, fresh and cool, lace is the perfect choice for a romantic bedroom, whether it is handmade filet crochet, antique lace or a modern machine made version.*

S unlight or moonlight shining through decorative lace curtains has a magical effect, casting an intricate pattern across the whole bedroom and creating a dreamy mood. Occasionally a gentle breeze may billow the drapes, sending the pattern on a shimmering dance.

More practically, lace curtains brighten a bedroom in winter by letting weak daylight through, while in summer they filter out harsh light, creating a soft, diffused effect.

On the bed itself there is nothing fresher than traditional crisp white linen edged with lace frills. And covering a plain coloured duvet or blanket with a fine lace bedspread allows a hint of colour to show through, highlighting the lace pattern.

A lace curtain with a clearly defined border makes an attractive bed throw or a casual floor length tablecloth. Use lace edging and appliqué to decorate soft furnishings such as cushions and towels.

Accessories such as nightdress cases, coat hangers, tissue box covers and scented sachets are just some of the things you can transform with lacy edging.

*Buttercup yellow walls provide the perfect backdrop for frothy lace at the window and embroidered cutwork bedlinen. The lace theme continues with crocheted lace edging on the bedside tablecloth.*

▶ *The creamy antique* lace bedspread introduces a feminine note and softens the lines of the wrought iron furniture in this sophisticated scheme. The choice of cream rather than white is a perfect complement to the delicate blush of rose in the walls and carpet.

▼ *Lace marries well* with florals and this cream based rose print is the perfect partner for ruffles of natural lace. Use lace trimmed accessories like these to introduce the lace theme to your existing scheme.

▶ *Crisp white bedlinen* detailed with Battenburg lace makes this cottage bedroom look cool and inviting. A bedside table is also dressed in similar lace finery. The blue carpet is an inspired choice, as it shows off the lacework to perfection.

◀ *Touches of lace* add a pretty accent to bedroom accessories. Dress plain white cotton lingerie bags with crocheted lace trims or display a piece of tape lace on a tissue box cover.

# CUTWORK WINDOW PANELS

*Decorative cutwork panels are ideal for window hangings, as light filters through the holes to highlight the embroidery. Choose an all-over design or just work a simple repeat edging motif for a plain blind.*

Cutwork is an embroidery technique in which the design is worked with buttonhole stitches and then selected areas around and between the shapes are cut away. You can work cutwork by hand or machine and it is generally stitched in white threads on white fabric, although a coloured thread with a slight sheen can be used to highlight the embroidery.

Designs can be simple shapes or more elaborate motifs, with large areas of cut-work joined with lace-like embroidered bars. The patterns need to be planned with care as the positions of the cut areas and worked bars are as important as the embroidered outlines.

For the simplest of window treatments using cutwork embroidery, just drape two cutwork mats or runners over a pole – it can be a wooden stick or metal rod. Or make up a plain roller blind and embroider the cut-work along the base edge.

*Two cutwork runners are cleverly combined to create an unusual semi-cover for a window. They are simply draped over a pole and secured by creating an informal casing with a few invisible stitches.*

# CUTWORK PANEL

You can decorate the lower edge of a plain, white cotton window panel or blind with a row of cutwork motifs stitched in a pastel cotton pearl thread. Use a machine zigzag stitch or embroider by hand using buttonhole stitch and stem stitch. Larger cut areas are held together by bars of buttonhole stitches.

You can make the panel as a fixed window dressing and make a cased heading to thread on to a curtain pole or rod, or make up the panel as a roller blind. For a blind, buy a kit to the exact measurement or the next size up and cut the pole to fit. For a crisp finish, you can spray the stitched panel with spray starch or fabric stiffener before hanging it in place.

trace motif

stitch diagram

**1 Measuring up** Fix the pole or blind brackets in place. Measure the width of the window recess. Measure the length of the pole or roller and the drop to the sill. Cut a piece of fabric to this measurement, adding 4cm (1½in) to the width for side hems and 17cm (6¾in) to the length. Mark the centre of the fabric on one short edge. Press the fabric.

**2 Tracing off the motifs** Cut a 20cm (8in) wide strip of tracing paper to the same width as the finished panel. Measure and mark a line 2cm (¾in) up from the bottom edge along the length of the tracing paper and mark the centre of this line. Trace off the motif, matching the centre of the tracing paper to the dotted line of the motif and aligning the bottom of the motif with the marked line.

**3 Fitting the design motifs** Continue to mark motifs across the whole strip, ending with a complete motif at each side if possible. If not, for a neat finish on each side, mark a buttonhole stitching line to reach from the last complete motif along to the side hem.

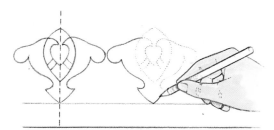

**4 Making up the transfer** Turn the tracing over and mark over the design lines with the transfer pencil. Make sure you follow the design lines exactly.

**5 Marking the fabric** With fabric right side up, place the tracing centrally over the base of the panel, matching the edge of the paper to the edge of the fabric and pin to hold. Press with an iron to transfer the design outlines on to the fabric. Remove the tracing.

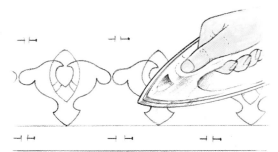

**6 Embroidering the design** Following the stitch diagram and key, work round the design outlines with stem stitch and buttonhole stitch. Make sure that the knotted edges of the buttonhole stitches always lie against the edges of the areas to be cut away.

**7 Cutting away the fabric** When all the stem and buttonhole stitching is complete, carefully cut away all the shaded areas shown on the trace motif. Work from the wrong side using small sharp-pointed scissors. Make sure that you do not accidentally cut away any of the stitch threads.

◣ *The trace motif (top) shows the cutwork design outline and the areas to be cut away. The stitch diagram (above) shows the main outline worked in buttonhole stitch and the linking twisted bars.*

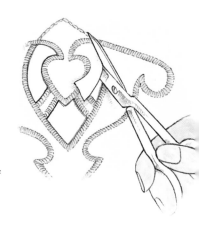

**8** **Adding twisted bars** Following the stitch diagram, work twisted bars at marked positions. Take the thread across the space, then twist the same thread back over the bridge to the starting point, keeping the twists even. Secure the thread end behind the buttonhole stitches.

**9** **Completing motif design** At the base of each cutwork motif, work a branch filling stitch. Take a stitch from **A**, diagonally to the right at **B**. Twist the thread twice round the main thread and then take a stitch diagonally to the left at **C**. Pass the thread over the main thread, under the right-hand branch, over the left-hand branch and under the main thread, as shown. Pass over and under the three branches once more to complete the knot. Twist the thread round the main branch the required number of times back to point **A**.

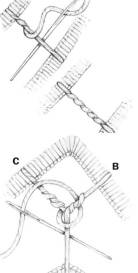

**10** **Finishing the blind** When the embroidery is complete, press from the wrong side, taking care not to flatten the stitches. Neaten and turn under 2cm (¾in) hems at the side edges and stitch in place. Stitch a casing if required. Stiffen the fabric and fit the panel on to the pole or roller and hang.

# CUTWORK WINDOW SCREEN

The perfect way to appreciate the decorative cutwork embroidery on a lovely old tablecloth is to use it as a screen. Simply draped over a frame, the embroidery is displayed to maximum effect. The needlework can be further enhanced by placing the screen in front of a window where the light can filter through the embroidery.

To create this effect you will need either three separate tablecloths, or one large one cut into three lengths. Alternatively, you can adapt a plain length of fabric or a white sheet by stitching on a cutwork border along the top edge.

To cover a screen in this way, measure the width and length of each panel and add about 25cm (10in) to the length to allow for a fabric overhang and 8cm (3in) to the width for double side hems. Cut out the panels to these measurements following the straight grain.

On each panel, turn in the side edges to form double 2cm (¾in) wide hems; pin and stitch. Then turn up and stitch a double 2cm (¾in) hem along the base edge in the same way.

To hang the panels, drape the cutwork edge of one fabric panel, right side out, over the top rod of the screen. Position the panels so the hems stand clear of the base. To hold the fabric securely, attach a strip of double-sided tape along the top of the rod.

*Create a classically elegant accessory with a cutwork panelled screen, and use it as an imaginative alternative to window drapes or blinds.*

# LACE AT THE WINDOW

*Sunlight gently filtering through the intricate stitchery of lace is a beautiful and soothing sight, and its subtle elegance adds grace and charm to all kinds of colour schemes and styles.*

R estrained and delicate, lavishly grand or country fresh – the appeal of lace is timeless and varied. Its traditions are rooted deep in history, developing across Europe over the centuries into a myriad of different styles and designs. The painstaking handwork is now efficiently reproduced by modern technology, so the filigree tracery of lace is an affordable luxury; but panels of antique lace are still to be found, and treasured as an investment.

Lace at the window brings many qualities to a room – not least privacy without the loss of precious light. Sunlight shining through lace softly dapples the room with shadow, and the special beauty of the fabric adds subtle texture and detail. Lace curtains, a standard feature in Edwardian and Victorian homes, are the perfect way to complete a period look, either draped in generous folds or hung in panels. The Scandinavian way with lace is often to create a pretty drapery over the window, dressing it but not impeding the light. And for a breezy country cottage effect, a faint flutter of lace at the window is always a charming touch.

Try contrasting the dainty fragility of lace with other harder textures such as marble, sun-bleached wood or old worn leather for an interesting effect. Huge natural jute tiebands, or chunky metal chain, emphasize the intricate delicacy of the fabric; flowers in sparkling glass or crystal bowls make flattering accessories. Use lace for its delicious detail in cool, all-white or creamy neutral schemes; alternatively, contrast it with rich jewel colours for a sense of sheer opulence.

*The classic cottage casement window is not complete without pretty lace curtains. Here, pure white, rose-strewn Nottingham lace drapes have frills and an added valance to frame the view invitingly. From outside they make a striking contrast to the black painted window frame.*

▶ *An antique panel* of cream guipure lace
accentuates the sense of a cherished past. The
lace has been loosely pleated and casually fixed,
and finishes short of the windowsill – an
unpretentious, confident arrangement that
blends precisely with the stripped wood frame
and burnished candlesticks.

◣ *A diamond pattern* in the lace panel at the
window of this cool Shaker-style room echoes the floor
design and the floral trellis on the sofa in the next
room. Links like this help to give a sense of calm and
order, even when colours and designs are bold. The
panel is simply hung by loops from pegs.

▶ *Summer wedding splendour*
adorns this window, with creamy
bridal lace lavishly cascading to the
floor from a simple cotton valance.
The design has an intricate all-
over pattern of arabesques and
whorls which give a rich texture,
and even the chair seats are
dressed for the occasion in frilly
mobcaps of the same lace.

# CURTAINED CUPBOARDS

*For storage with style, curtained cupboards give a room a well furnished look. The effect can be charming and homey, or supremely elegant, depending on the fabric you choose.*

Closed cupboards, whether they are built in or free standing, can be overpowering or merely featureless. One way of remedying the situation is to substitute solid doors for glazed ones. But if you don't want your possessions either on view or exposed to sunlight, curtaining provides an excellent alternative.

Choice of fabric is critical. Material should be fairly lightweight; upholstery fabric is too heavy to pleat up properly and too bulky to fit neatly inside a door. Small-scale prints in muted colours are more effective than bold, vividly coloured patterns which attract too much attention. Provençal patterns, fine stripes or checks, gingham and toile de Jouy are all eminently suitable.

The classic treatment is to hang the fabric on the inside of the door so that it forms a finely pleated screen. Fit narrow rods or covered wire at the top and bottom of the door frame and shirr the fabric along the rods by means of cased channels or headings. Alternatively, the fabric can be fixed to hang flat against the frame. It's important in either case to ensure the material is secured both at the top and the bottom so that the curtains hang neatly.

Curtaining cupboards can take the place of glazing or be used in conjunction with it. In a variation on the same theme you can partner curtaining with wire mesh – such as chicken wire – for a more rustic, country-style effect.

*Curtained cupboards flank open display shelves for distinctive kitchen storage. The sunny floral print complements the yellow walls, creating a charming, light effect.*

◀ *For a unified scheme,* coordinate cupboard curtains with window curtains. This bold striped material looks equally good gathered at the window as it does hung flat behind the open door panels. The strong geometric shape of the fretwork sets off the effect.

▶ *A built-in cupboard* can be obtrusive in a traditional or period-style sitting room; fabric instead of solid doors softens the effect. Subtle toile de Jouy makes an elegant statement in a formal room.

◀ *Simple cotton* in a monochrome check hides the contents of an armoire and harmonizes with the graphic black and white colour scheme. Hanging fabric on the inside of cupboard doors helps to keep possessions in good condition, protected from the harmful effects of direct light.

# LINING CUPBOARDS

*Fabric and paper linings add instant decorative lift to cupboards and alcoves and offer an opportunity for creating an inexpensive yet stylish showcase for displaying ornaments and mementoes.*

Though shelves and drawers are often lined for practical reasons, it's simple to take the idea a step further by using a stylish lining material as an eye-catching decorative feature. A well chosen lining added to open- or glass-fronted shelves or cupboards can create a handsome backdrop to a display and a final design flourish in a room. A closed cupboard needn't be excluded from these creative touches – not only will the cupboard be a pleasure to open, but you can also leave the door slightly ajar to reveal the stylish interior more of the time.

Choose either a fabric, a wallcovering or a paper lining – you're likely to need only a small amount,

so you may be able to make use of a remnant of fabric or wallcovering left over from a previous decorating project. Otherwise, look for a bargain in discontinued lines, or treat yourself to something special that would be too expensive for anything but a small-scale project such as this.

Washable wallcoverings or PVC-coated fabrics are best for areas that need frequent wiping, such as kitchen shelves. Otherwise choose a fairly sturdy fabric or wallcovering. A small-scale pattern works better than a large one. Look for a colour and pattern that blend well as a backdrop but also suit the general setting – you can even reinforce a theme with, say, an herb print in a kitchen.

*Using colour as a visual link is one of the simplest ways to create a successful display. Here, lining a plain cupboard interior with peach and honey coloured striped wallpaper makes a stunning backdrop for a collection of earth-toned tableware.*

# FABRIC LININGS

Choose fabric that's medium- to heavyweight, and closely woven, so it won't stretch out of shape, and is firm enough to withstand gluing and stapling. Avoid very lightweight and sheer fabrics, as their delicacy is lost against a solid surface and the adhesive is likely to seep through and spoil the front of the fabric.

First decide on which parts of the alcove or cupboard you want to line. Lining the back of the alcove or cupboard is easiest if you first remove the shelves; if this isn't possible, you'll need to make separate linings to fit between the shelves. If necessary, paint any unlined area to complement the lining. Measure up the areas to be lined, allowing for pattern matching and for displaying patterns. Add an extra 2.5cm (1in) for turnings at the edges of the lined areas.

## MATERIALS

For simplicity and a smooth finish, use spray adhesive to stick the fabric in position then peel back the edges and reinforce their grip with a small amount of PVA adhesive. Always be sure to work in a well ventilated room when you are using spray adhesive.

▶ *To emphasize the interesting arrangement of this alcove shelving, only the back wall is lined with fabric – white painted shelves standing out in stark contrast to the dark chequered lining.*

### YOU WILL NEED

- ❖ SCREWDRIVER and ABRASIVE PAPER (optional)
- ❖ PAINT AND DECORATORS' BRUSH (optional)
- ❖ FABRIC
- ❖ TAPE MEASURE and SCISSORS
- ❖ SPRAY ADHESIVE
- ❖ PVA ADHESIVE
- ❖ STIFF BRISTLED ARTISTS' BRUSH
- ❖ PAPER and MASKING TAPE
- ❖ STAPLE GUN and STAPLES

**1 Preparing the cupboard (optional)** Remove the shelves and unscrew any supporting battens or brackets. Sand the battens smooth and paint to coordinate with the lining fabric or leave them for covering with fabric.

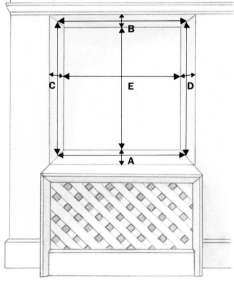

**2 Cutting out fabric** Measure the height and width of each area being covered – base (**A**), top (**B**), sides (**C** and **D**) and back (**E**). Make a note of the measurements adding 2.5cm (1in) all round for turnings. Cut out fabric panels to these sizes, arranging any obvious patterns as appropriate. Mark and cut out a 2.5cm (1in) square in each corner of each panel.

**3 Lining the base and top** Press under 2.5cm (1in) along the front edge of panels **A** and **B**. Spray adhesive generously over the base of the cupboard or alcove and fit the fabric into position with the pressed edge at the front. Smooth the fabric so the cut-out squares fit into the corners and the turnings extend equally around the back and sides. Line the top in the same way.

**4 Securing the edges** Carefully peel back the pressed edges and turnings around the sides of the base and top lining, Using an artists' brush, apply a small amount of PVA adhesive to the cupboard or alcove walls underneath and press the edges firmly back into place.

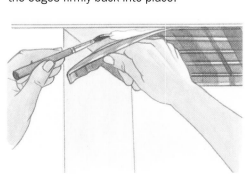

**Fitting the back panel** Press under 2.5cm (1in) along each edge of panel **E**. Mask off the side panels and spray adhesive over the back wall. Smooth the panel into position then peel back the pressed edges and reinforce with PVA adhesive, as before.

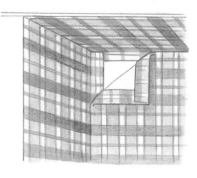

**Cutting out the shelf fabric** For each shelf, cut out a rectangle of fabric to fit tightly around the four sides with an overlap at the back edge and allowing for a 2.5cm (1in) turning at the side edges.

**Covering the shelves** Press under a 2.5cm (1in) turning at the sides of the shelf panels. For each shelf, use staples to attach one raw edge of a fabric panel to the back edge of the shelf. Wrap the fabric around the shelf and secure the remaining raw edge so the pressed edges line up with the shelf side edges and the fabric is tight but not stretched.

**Fitting the battens and shelves (optional)** Cover the battens with fabric if desired. If necessary, make a small hole in the fabric at the screw hole positions then screw the battens back in place. Replace the shelves so the stapled edges are at the back.

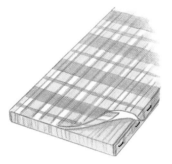

**Lining the sides** Press under 2.5cm (1in) along the top, bottom and front edges of panels **C** and **D**. Mask off the top and base linings with paper and masking tape. Spray adhesive over the side wall then smooth the appropriate panel into place, so the pressed edges line up with the top, bottom and front of the side wall and a 2.5cm (1in) turning extends on to the back wall. Repeat for the other side and reinforce edges with PVA adhesive as before.

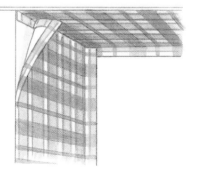

▶ *Fabric woven with a trompe l'oeil design of leather-bound tomes is perfect for lining a bookcase.*

# PAPER LININGS

For a very smooth finish and even quicker results, paper makes a good alternative to fabric for lining cupboards and shelves. Ideally you need to use a mediumweight paper that is easy to work with but will not tear when dampened with adhesive. Wallpaper, heavier weight gift wrap, old maps and even parcel paper are all suitable; or you could create a collage using old maps, music sheets or book pages.

If the shelving is in constant use and the paper is likely to become grubby, use a washable wallpaper cover with sheets of sticky back plastic or apply two or three coats of a clear matt polyurethane varnish.

The technique for lining with paper is similar to that for fabric; however, because the paper does not fray there's no need to add a pressing allowance along the front edges of the top and bottom panel; the top, bottom and front edges of the side panels and all edges of the back panel. Paste the wrong side of the paper with PVA or wallpaper adhesive and stick in position, using a wallpaper brush or soft rag to smooth out any bubbles gently. If using wallpaper, allow to soak after pasting for at least ten minutes so the paper is easier to handle.

Finally, wrap the shelves in paper or cut paper panels large enough to cover the top of the shelf plus extra for a decorative shaped overlap.

▲ *A patterned gift wrap of cactus all-in-a-row lends itself to a cutwork shelf trim. To prevent the paper curling up at the edges, mount it on a piece of cardboard with spray adhesive before cutting out the shapes. Then stick the cardboard and paper on to the shelf edge.*

◀ *Larder shelves lined with wipe-clean wallpaper are a pretty and practical solution for kitchen storage. To form the scalloped trim, allow for an overlap at the front edge of each shelf lining then draw semi-circles side by side along the overlap using a cup as a template. Cut out the scallops and stick the lining to the shelf so the shaped edge hangs over the front.*

# QUICK CHAIR COVERS

*Slip-on seat and back covers are a quick way to dress up ordinary dining chairs to make them into a special feature, and to breathe new life into battered kitchen chairs.*

Whether you have an uninspiring set of dining chairs, a motley collection of battered kitchen chairs or a single jarring bedroom chair, slip-on covers are a simple and relatively inexpensive way to give them all a smart new image. The covers sit on the seat and/or back of the chair only – so they're easier to make than all-enclosing loose covers and require less fabric. They're simply tied or buttoned in place, so you can whip them off in an instant for laundering or a refreshing change of scene.

Make the covers from mediumweight furnishing fabric, and give them a stamp of individuality with clever detailing. Shape the hems into quirky zigzags, soft scallops or waves or even heraldic shields. Add a jaunty touch with a frilled or pleated skirt; as a change from ribbon ties, attach the covers with dainty rouleaux loops and self-cover buttons, fluffy butterfly bows, military frogging or wooden toggles slipped through jute loops. If you want to machine wash the covers, pre-shrink the fabric before sewing.

*Zigzagged hems add a zany touch to the slip-on back and seat covers that dress this old dining chair. Designing your own covers is a great way to exercise your creative talents and put an individual stamp on a room.*

# MAKING SLIP-ON COVER PATTERNS

These steps show how to make matching slip-on seat and back covers for a dining chair. The back cover has a gusset to ensure a good fit, and is tied in place with ribbons – or you could make self-fabric ties if you prefer. The seat cover has a wadded top for added softness, and a crisply scalloped skirt; it's fixed in place with Velcro spots, topped with decorative self-cover buttons. Both covers are piped for a defined edge. Take 1.5cm (⅝in) seam allowances throughout.

▶ *A neat tie-on back cover and a scallop-skirted seat cover, both in a fresh check, add Scandinavian style to a dining chair.*

**1 Making the main back pattern** Lay the chair on its back and place a sheet of paper over the back. Use the pencil to draw along the sides and top of the chair back on to the paper. Mark a straight line across the bottom of the pattern where you want the cover to finish. Cut out the paper pattern, adding a 1.5cm (⅝in) seam allowance to the side edges and a 2.5cm (1in) hem allowance to the base edge. Check the fit on the chair.

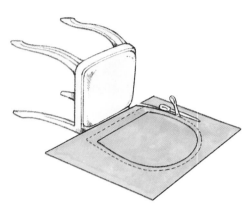

**2 Measuring for the back gusset** To find the gusset length, use a piece of cord to measure from the base edge on the main back pattern, up and around the sides and back to the base, including the hem allowance. For the gusset width, measure the thickness of the chair back at its thickest point. Add 3cm (1¼in) to both measurements.

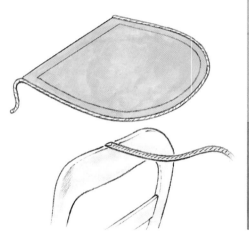

**3 Making the seat pattern** Lay a piece of newspaper or brown paper on the chair seat and mark with a pencil right along the seat edge. Snip into the paper for ease as necessary where the chair back struts meet the seat, and mark around these. Add a 1.5cm (⅝in) seam allowance all round and cut out the paper pattern. Make sure you check the fit carefully.

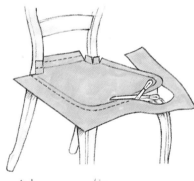

**4 Making the front skirt pattern** Measure from one back corner of the seat, around the front to the other back corner. Add 10cm (4in) for two back overlaps. Cut paper this length by 15cm (6in) wide. Make a scallop template from card and use it to shape one long edge of the pattern, with a whole scallop to each side of the corners.

**5 Making the back skirt pattern** Measure across the back edge of the chair and add 3cm (1¼in) for seam allowances. Cut a piece of paper this length by 15cm (6in) wide. Use the scallop template to shape one long edge of the pattern, matching the scallop positions to those on the front of the skirt.

**6 Cutting out** *From furnishing fabric* Cut two main back pieces, one back gusset, one seat, two skirt fronts and two skirt backs. *From wadding and calico* Cut one seat pattern.

# Making up the Covers

**1** **Trimming back gusset** Make piping to trim both long gusset edges and all seat edges. Cut ribbon into 12 lengths. Matching raw edges, pin a pair of ribbons 2.5cm (1in) in from each gusset end on the right side. Pin two more pairs at 5cm (2in) intervals in from the first pair at each end. Right sides facing and raw edges matching, stitch piping to each long gusset edge, catching in ribbons.

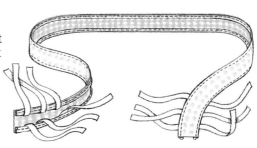

**2** **Making up the back cover** Fold the gusset in half widthways to find the centre, and mark with a pin. Repeat to find the centre top of the main back pieces. With right sides together and matching the centre marks, pin and stitch the gusset to the sides and top of first one then the other main back piece, easing to fit round curves or corners.

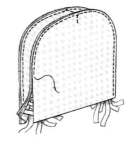

**3** **Finishing the back cover** Trim and neaten the raw edges. Press under and stitch a double 12mm (½in) hem along the base edge of the cover. Turn the cover right side out and slip it over the chair. Tie the ribbons, gathering in any fullness.

**4** **Piping the seat** Right side up, lay main fabric seat over the wadding seat; pin and tack together. Right sides together and raw edges matching, stitch piping round the edge of main fabric, clipping it for ease at corners and joining the ends at the back edge.

**5** **Stitching the scalloped edgings** Lay the two front skirt pieces right sides together. Pin and stitch along the short ends and scalloped edge, following the curves and pivoting the fabric on the needle at points. Snip the seam allowances at the points and at intervals along the curves. Turn the skirt right side out and press. Repeat for the back skirt pieces.

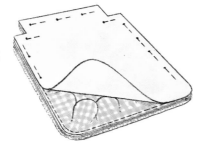

**6** **Attaching the skirt** Fold the skirts in half widthways to find the centre points and mark them with a pin. Repeat to mark the centre front and back of the piped seat. With the right sides together and matching the marks, pin the front skirt to the seat up to the back corner cut-outs. Stitch the skirt in place. Snip into the seam allowance at the end of the stitching, turn in the remaining raw edges and slipstitch closed. Repeat to stitch the back skirt in place.

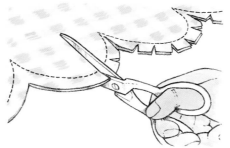

**7** **Lining the seat cover** Fold the skirt in to lie over the right side of the seat; pin to secure. Right sides together and edges matching, lay the calico seat on top and stitch round edges, leaving a gap in the back. Turn right side out and press. Slipstitch gap closed.

**8** **Adding the fastenings** Cover the buttons following the manufacturer's instructions. Stitch three buttons in a vertical row to the two outer edges of the back skirt, on the right side. Stitch one half of a touch-and-close spot on the wrong side beneath each button, and the other halves to correspond on the right side of the front skirt overlaps. Slip the cover over the seat and press the fastenings together.

# SEAT COVERS WITH GATHERED SKIRT

Soften the lines of dining chairs by making slip-on seat covers with full, gathered skirts. The weight of the skirt should hold the cover in place, but if you find it shifts you can secure it by adding fabric or ribbon ties at the back struts.

You will need about 1m (1⅛yd) of furnishing fabric for each chair cover; or, if you are using a contrasting fabric for the skirt as shown here, you will need about 50cm (⅝yd) for the seat and 60cm (¾yd) for the skirt. Allow extra if you are making self-piping.

*These frilled seat covers are made from two toning fabrics – an elegant purple and ivory toile de Jouy on the seat and a plain cream cotton for the skirt. For a perfect fit on the carver (the chair with arms), the cover is neatly shaped around the arm rails as well as the back struts.*

**1 Cutting out the seat** Make a pattern for the seat as in *Making Slip-on Cover Patterns*, step 3. Cut one seat from main fabric, one from wadding and one from calico.

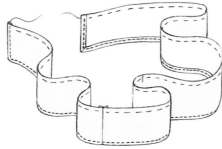

**2 Cutting out the skirt** For the front skirt, measure round the seat from one back corner to the other, and double the measurement. Cut and join enough 20cm (8in) wide strips to make up a piece this length. For the back skirt, measure across the back of the seat, between the struts, and double the measurement. Cut a 20cm (8in) wide fabric strip this length.

**3 Piping and gathering** Pad and pipe the seat as in *Making up the Covers*, step 4. On the lower and side edges of the skirts, press under and stitch a double 1cm (⅜in) hem. Mark the centre top edge of both skirt pieces, then run a gathering thread along the top edges. Mark the centre front and back of the seat.

**4 Assembling the cover** With right sides together, pin the front skirt to the seat at the centre front point and at the back corners, pull up the gathers and adjust to fit. Stitch the skirt in place. Repeat with the back skirt. Line the cover with calico as for *Making up the Covers*, step 7.

# RE-COVERING DROP-IN SEATS

*Covering a drop-in seat pad is a simple upholstery task which makes the world of difference to worn or tired looking dining and side chairs.*

A s their name suggests, drop-in seat pads can be eased in and out of their frames without difficulty, making re-covering them one of the least cumbersome of upholstery tasks. Their simple shape – usually square, though some have cut-away corners to accommodate chair legs – is another factor in their favour, as is the small amount of fabric required to restore their good looks – about 80cm (32in) for each seat.

Select a strong, hardwearing, medium to heavyweight fabric for the new covers. Damask or a needlepoint-effect is ideal for formal settings, while modern checks or stripes work well in rooms with a more casual feel. Save luxurious fabrics for side or bedroom chairs which aren't subject to such heavy wear. Always apply a layer of wadding underneath the fabric to smooth out any unevenness in the pad filling. It's also a good idea to spray the finished seat with a fabric protector to help repel spills.

If your chair seats aren't worn or grubby enough to justify re-covering but you fancy a change, consider making temporary slip-over covers which are held in place with a draw-string casing on the underside.

*With a coat of white paint and a newly covered drop-in seat in a checked leaf print, this chair is given a smart face lift to suit the country-style decor.*

# RE-COVERING A DROP-IN SEAT PAD

A *traditional drop-in seat pad* comprises various layers of fabric and stuffing which give the seat its firm but comfy shape – generally strips of webbing stretched over the frame, topped with layers of hessian, hair stuffing, calico, wadding and finally the top fabric cover. More *modern chair seat pads* are often simply padded with foam over a hardboard base, then covered with wadding and a top fabric.

To remove old upholstery materials – a process known in the trade as 'taking down' or 'ripping out' – you can invest in a ripping chisel (for removing tacks) or a staple remover; however, for a relatively straightforward project like a drop-in seat, you'll find an old screwdriver serves just as well. When removing tacks, use these tools in conjunction with a wooden mallet. When removing

the old cover, be sure to take off only the bottoming cloth, if present (this is sometimes added on traditional pads to give a neat finish), the top fabric cover and the wadding.

If you find the pad underneath is in poor condition, either take it to a specialist to be re-upholstered or tackle the job yourself with the aid of a reliable upholstery guide. In the case of modern foam pads, just take the seat to a foam supplier who will cut a new piece of foam to shape for you.

These instructions are for re-covering a pad using a hammer and tacks; you can use a heavy duty staple gun and staples instead, but this doesn't allow as much freedom to make adjustments as you work. It's a good idea to clean and polish the wooden frame before replacing the re-covered pad.

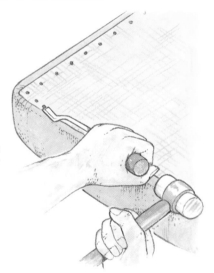

| YOU WILL NEED |
| --- |
| ❖ WOODEN MALLET AND RIPPING CHISEL, STAPLE REMOVER OR OLD SCREWDRIVER |
| ❖ PLIERS (optional) |
| ❖ BRUSH for cleaning pad |
| ❖ TAPE MEASURE |
| ❖ POLYESTER WADDING |
| ❖ FURNISHING FABRIC |
| ❖ SCISSORS |
| ❖ HAMMER AND 16mm (⅝in) UPHOLSTERY TACKS OR STAPLE GUN AND STAPLES |
| ❖ FIRMLY WOVEN FABRIC for covering base (optional) |
| ❖ SPRAY-ON FABRIC PROTECTOR (optional) |

## REMOVING THE OLD SEAT COVER

**1** **Removing tacks and staples** Push the pad up out of the frame from below. Working in the direction of the wood grain to avoid splitting the wood, remove the necessary tacks or staples as follows:
*Using a ripping chisel* (for tacks) Lodge the chisel under the head of the tack; strike it with a sharp blow with a mallet as you flick the chisel upward, as shown here.
*Using a staple remover* Slide the head of the staple remover under the staple; gently lever it out of the seat frame or base.
*Using a screwdriver* Slide the head of the screwdriver underneath the tack head; hammer gently with the mallet, easing the tack out of the wood. You can also use a screwdriver to lever out staples.

**2** **Dealing with stubborn tacks** If the tacks or staples are firmly embedded in the frame, cut away the fabric around them to make space underneath for the chisel, staple remover or screwdriver. Use pliers to remove any headless tacks.

**3** **Cleaning the pad** When you have removed all the tacks or staples securing the bottoming cloth (if present), the top fabric cover and the wadding, pull these off. Inspect the pad and brush it to remove dust.

## APPLYING THE NEW SEAT COVER

**1** **Cutting out wadding** Measure across the seat pad both ways from front to back and side to side, from the base edge on one side, over the top and down to the base edge on the opposite side. Cut a piece of wadding to this size plus 1.5cm (⅝in) all round, and lay it centrally over the pad. Measure and mark the centre of each side of the drop-in seat, on the underside.

**2** **Adding the fabric** Cut a piece of fabric to the measurements taken plus 5cm (2in) all round, centring any motifs and with the grain running lengthways on the seat pad from front to back. Fold the fabric in half in both directions to find the centre point on each edge and firmly pinch the edges to mark. Lay the fabric right side up over the wadding, lining up the marked centre points on the seat and fabric.

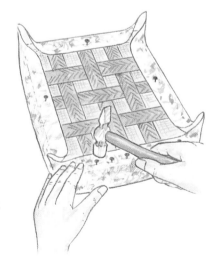

**3** **Temporary tacking** Turn the pad upside down and pull the fabric to the back, pulling it taut but not stretching it. Knock a tack *halfway* into the frame in the centre of each edge. Starting at the front edge and working out from the central tack, temporarily tack the fabric in place in this way, spacing the tacks about 4cm (1½in) apart. Repeat at back edge. Check the fabric is straight and repeat at side edges, leaving corners free.

**4** **Tacking off** Turn the pad over and check that the fabric is straight and taut over the seat. Adjust if necessary, then hammer the tacks home, making sure the heads lie flat so the tacks anchor soundly and won't cut through the fabric.

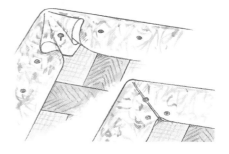

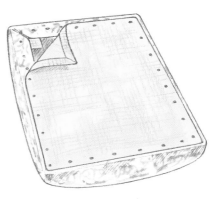

**5** **Tacking the corners** At each corner open out the fabric, pull it to the underside and secure with a temporary tack. Tuck under excess fabric on each side, forming a neat mitre, and tack in place. Remove the temporary tack or hammer it in. Trim off any excess. Treat cut-away corners on seats shaped to accommodate the chair legs in same way, drawing the fabric right into the indent, then neatly tucking the excess under at each side.

**6** **Neatening (optional)** Lay the pad right way up on the base cloth and draw round it. Cut out, adding 2cm (¾in) all round. Press under 2.5cm (1in) all round and tack the cloth to the base of the pad to cover all raw edges and protect the pad from dust. Spray the seat with fabric protector if desired.

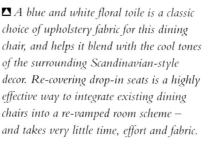

◤ *A blue and white floral toile is a classic choice of upholstery fabric for this dining chair, and helps it blend with the cool tones of the surrounding Scandinavian-style decor. Re-covering drop-in seats is a highly effective way to integrate existing dining chairs into a re-vamped room scheme — and takes very little time, effort and fabric.*

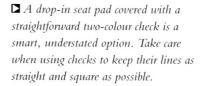

▶ *A drop-in seat pad covered with a straightforward two-colour check is a smart, understated option. Take care when using checks to keep their lines as straight and square as possible.*

# QUICK SEAT COVERS

In honour of a special dinner party, or just for a refreshing change, you can make slip-on covers for drop-in seat pads, held in place on the underside with a draw-string. As the covers are only temporary, feel free to use more exotic fabrics; you could even use a different fabric for each chair for a lively colour and pattern mix. Remember that you're adding an extra fabric layer to a pad that's already covered, so avoid bulky fabrics or you may have trouble fitting the seat back into the chair frame.

| YOU WILL NEED |
| --- |
| ❖ LIGHTWEIGHT FABRIC |
| ❖ DRESSMAKERS' PENCIL |
| ❖ SCISSORS |
| ❖ PINS |
| ❖ MATCHING SEWING THREAD |
| ❖ NARROW TAPE OR CORD |
| ❖ BODKIN OR LARGE SAFETY PIN |

**1 Cutting out the cover** Push the pad out of the chair frame from underneath. Lay the fabric out flat, with the wrong side up, and place the pad on top. Draw around the outside of the pad with a dressmakers' pencil. Cut out adding 10cm (4in) all round.

☑ *Temporary covers for drop-in seat pads give you the freedom to use highly original and luxurious fabrics – like this star-sprinkled purple silk, classically influenced Grecian urn print or richly coloured maroon and purple silk tartan.*

**2 Forming a casing** Press 1cm (⅜in), then 2cm (¾in) to the wrong side all round the cover fabric. To mitre the corners, unfold the larger hem, press in each corner across the corner point, then refold the larger hem. Stitch the hem in place close to the inner edge, leaving a 5cm (2in) opening at the centre back.

## TIP
### TIME-SAVING PATTERN
**If you're making covers for a set of identical dining chairs, use the fabric piece cut out in step 1 as a pattern for all the other chairs.**

**3 Threading the cord** Thread the bodkin or safety pin with cord or tape long enough to go all round the casing plus 20cm (8in). Feed the tape round the casing, leaving both ends loose at the centre back.

**4 Fitting the cover** Lay the cover centrally over the seat pad with right side uppermost. Pull the cord or tape ends to gather up the cover round the seat pad. Tie the cord or tape ends together securely in a bow. Finally, push the covered seat pad back into the chair frame.

# PIPED SQUAB CUSHION

*A wonderful way to make your kitchen look cosier and your hard wooden dining chairs feel more comfortable is to kit them out with some tie-on seat pads covered in a bright, cheerful fabric.*

A squab cushion is a fitted cushion, tailored for a hard seat such as a kitchen chair or bench. It primarily provides more comfortable seating but, when made up in a bold pattern or bright fabric that coordinates with the rest of the colour scheme, it serves as a decorative accessory as well.

Neat squab cushions don't slip off or slide about the chair because they are tied in place round the back legs.

The style of slim, piped seat pad described here, without a zip or gusset, is the simplest to make.

*These soft, fully coordinated squab cushions are anchored to their seats with long ballerina ties.*

# MAKING THE CUSHION

### YOU WILL NEED

❖ NEWSPAPER
❖ PENCIL
❖ SCISSORS for paper
❖ TAPE MEASURE
❖ FABRIC for cover and ties – see steps 2 and 5
❖ Contrasting FABRIC for piping
❖ PIPING CORD
❖ SEWING THREAD, PINS
❖ 4CM (1½IN) thick SHEET FOAM
❖ FELT TIP PEN
❖ DRESSMAKER'S SCISSORS or CRAFT KNIFE

Since these cushions are likely to get a lot of wear, choose a strong, easily washable fabric for the covers so that you can keep them looking fresh and clean. The cushion pad itself is easy to cut to shape from sheet foam.

If you use a plain, coordinated fabric for the piping, your cushions will have a true designer's finish. Experiment with the length and width of the ties, and ways of fastening them too, to create all sorts of effects.

**1** **Making a pattern** To make a paper pattern, hold a large sheet of newspaper over the seat and mark round the edges with a pencil.

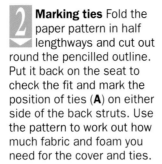

**2** **Marking ties** Fold the paper pattern in half lengthways and cut out round the pencilled outline. Put it back on the seat to check the fit and mark the position of ties (**A**) on either side of the back struts. Use the pattern to work out how much fabric and foam you need for the cover and ties.

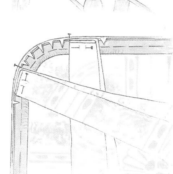

**3** **Cutting out** Pin the pattern on the wrong side of the fabric, making sure stripes or any pattern is well positioned and any large motif is centred. Cut out two cover pieces, adding 1.5cm (⅝in) all round as a seam allowance. Fix a pin into the edge of the fabric at each mark indicating the position of the ties.

**4** **Adding piping** Make sufficient covered piping to go all the way round the cover, adding 2cm (¾in) for joining. Starting at the centre of the back edge, pin and tack the piping round the right side of top cover piece, with raw edges matching. Snip into the piping seam allowance at curves. Join ends of piping centrally on back edge.

**5** **Making up ties** For each tie, cut a strip of fabric 74 x 22cm (29 x 8¾in). Fold in half lengthways with right sides together and cut across one short end at 45° to fold. Stitch down the side and across end, 1cm (⅜in) from the edge. Trim across corners and turn through. Push out the corners and press.

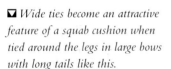

▼ *Wide ties become an attractive feature of a squab cushion when tied around the legs in large bows with long tails like this.*

**7** **Making up cover** Lay the under piece of the cover over the top, right sides together. Pin, tack and machine stitch round two sides and the front, leaving an opening along the back. Trim seam allowance, snip corners and turn to right side.

**6** **Attaching ties** Pleat the raw ends of the ties to a third of their width. Pin over the piping against the pins on either side of each back corner. Machine stitch in place, 1cm (⅜in) from the edge.

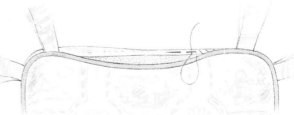

**8** **Cutting foam pad** Place the pattern on a piece of 4cm (1½in) thick foam and mark round with a felt tip pen. Cut out along line with sharp scissors or a craft knife.

**9** **Finishing off** Put the foam into the cover through the slit in the back. Fold in the opening edge and either slipstitch to close, or sew in strips of Velcro fastening and press closed.

# FITTED TABLE CLOTH

*Sleek and unpretentious, a fitted table cloth is a smart alternative to a standard cloth. With the skirt sliced to a practical mini-length, this stylish cloth is comfortable to sit at as well.*

Define the graceful lines of your circular or oval table with a chic fitted cloth. Made with a skirt in two complementary fabrics, and piped for a crisp edge around the tabletop, this cloth is smart enough to be a permanent addition to your room and can be made to coordinate handsomely with your other soft furnishings. If you have a valuable table, this is the ideal way to protect it. If it is, on the other hand, a little shabby, this cloth is a perfect disguise.

For the best results, use a mediumweight fabric for the body of the cloth – it needs to be crisp and firm enough to hold its shape

well. An all-over pattern, such as a check or stripe, works well for the panel around the hem, especially if it is cut on the bias as shown here – this works out to be quite economical if you are also making your own covered piping to match. Alternatively, if you want to use a directional design, the panel can be cut on the straight grain.

Check the width of the fabric before you buy it – the wider the better if you want to avoid seaming across the top of the cloth. You can adapt these instructions to make a square cover or scale down the size for a dainty cover to suit an occasional table.

*What does a well dressed table wear for afternoon tea? A fitted, short-cropped cloth in understated grey and white is a smart and original option.*

# MAKING THE TABLE CLOTH

## YOU WILL NEED

- ❖ PLAIN FURNISHING FABRIC
- ❖ PATTERNED FURNISHING FABRIC
- ❖ TAPE MEASURE
- ❖ SCISSORS
- ❖ MATCHING SEWING THREADS
- ❖ DRAWING PIN
- ❖ PATTERN PAPER
- ❖ PIPING CORD

These instructions are for the circular table cloth with a bias-cut border, shown on the previous page. To estimate how much fabric you need, measure the diameter of the table. You need this amount of plain fabric plus enough to make a 15cm (6in) deep skirt to fit around the edge of the table; allow extra if joining widths for the top piece. You need enough patterned fabric to make a 15cm (6in) deep, bias-cut strip and piping to fit round the table edge.

**1** **Measuring up** Measure the diameter of the table (**A**) and the circumference (**B**). Add 3cm (1¼in) to measurement **A** to give measurement **C**. If this measurement is greater than the width of your plain fabric you must join fabric widths to create the cloth's top piece. If your fabric is wide enough, cut a square measuring **C** x **C**, then go to step 3.

**2** **Joining widths** Cut one length of plain fabric measuring **C** by the width of the fabric. Subtract the width of the fabric from **C** and divide by two. Add 3cm (1¼in) to get measurement **D**. Cut two plain fabric rectangles to **C** by **D**. With right sides together, stitch one rectangle to each long edge of the larger, central panel. Press seams open.

**3** **Making a pattern** Fold the fabric square into quarters, matching the outer edges and seams. Cut a square of pattern paper to this size. Tie one end of a length of string around a pencil and use the drawing pin to secure the other end to the corner of the pattern paper, so that the length of taut string in-between is exactly half of measurement **C**. Holding the pencil upright, draw a quarter circle on the pattern paper.

**4** **Cutting out the top piece** Pin the paper pattern to the folded fabric, matching the right angle corner to the centre fabric fold. If the fabric is stable, cut round the paper pattern, through all thicknesses. If it is bulky or slippery, cut through each layer separately. Open out the fabric circle and press it flat.

**5** **Cutting out the skirt strips** *From plain fabric*, cut enough 15cm (6in) deep strips from across the width to make a strip to measurement **B** plus 3cm (1¼in). *From patterned fabric*, cut enough 15cm (6in) deep strips on the bias to make a strip to **B** plus 3cm (1¼in). Also cut enough bias strips to cover piping cord to the length of **B** plus 2cm (¾in). Make up the piping.

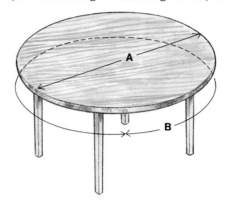

**6** **Stitching the skirt** On both long edges of the patterned strip press 5mm (¼in) to the wrong side. Fold the strip in half and pin the folded edges over one long edge of the plain fabric strip. Topstitch through all layers close to the fold. With right sides together, tack together the short ends of the joined strips to make a ring. Check the fit around the table, then stitch.

**7** **Assembling the cloth** With right sides facing, pin and tack the piping cord around the edge of the circular top piece, matching the raw edges. Neatly join the ends of the piping cord. With right sides together, tack the raw edge of the skirt to the raw edge of the circle, clipping into the seam allowance for ease. Stitch. Press the seams towards the skirt and neaten the raw edges.

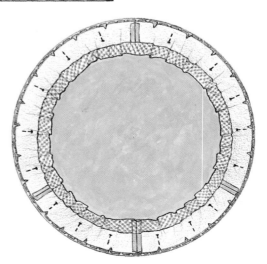

*You can easily adapt the instructions given here to make a cover for an occasional table, like this delightful floral cloth with a scalloped skirt.*

# EMBROIDERED TABLE LINEN

*Embroider delicately intertwining ivy leaves on to a table cloth and napkins for original and smart table linen. Use ready-made table linen or buy fabric to make your own.*

Trailing ivy leaves, worked in a combination of chain and stem stitch, are easy to embroider. You can use them to decorate table linen with a design that is both versatile and quick to work. The leaves, suggested by outline only, can be embroidered in any colour – so you can pick one to complement your tableware.

White or cream linen is a traditional choice for the cloth, yet there is no reason why you shouldn't embroider a darker colour – just use a paler embroidery cotton. For instance, for a festive occasion try embroidering a dramatic red or green cloth with silver or gold leaves.

You can work the design on to a cloth you have already, buy one for the purpose or make up a cloth from a plain, firmly woven cotton, linen or blend. The design is suitable for a square or rectangular cloth of any dimension. For a large cloth, you can embroider the design on each corner; for a smaller cloth you may only want to embroider one corner.

It is easy to adapt the design to a round cloth by rearranging the outline as you trace it off so that it gently curves into a garland shape. You can also enlarge or reduce the design on a photocopier to use the ivy motifs on other items, such as bedlinen.

*A simple ivy leaf design, embroidered in natural forest hues, takes little time to work and adds an individual touch to a crisp linen table cloth.*

# MAKING THE TABLE CLOTH

These instructions show how to make the table cloth and napkins yourself, but you can embroider ready-made ones if you prefer, provided they are made from a plain weave fabric, either in a synthetic mix or pure linen or cotton. If making the table linen yourself, measure up for the size and style of table cloth you require and cut it out, adding 4cm (1½in) all round for the hem.

For the best results when working the embroidery stitches, keep the fabric taut by mounting it in an embroidery hoop. Don't leave the fabric in the hoop too long, as it may become distorted or marked. To gauge the best size for the embroidery stitches, practise on a spare piece of fabric first. Instructions on how to work chain and stem stitch are given on page 93.

Instructions on how to work chain and stem stitch are given on page 93.

## YOU WILL NEED

❖ PLAIN WEAVE FABRIC for making the table linen, or READY-MADE TABLE CLOTH AND NAPKINS

❖ 2H PENCIL, RULER AND SET SQUARE

❖ TRACING PAPER

❖ DRESSMAKERS' CARBON PAPER

❖ MATCHING THREAD

❖ STRANDED EMBROIDERY COTTON – in the colours indicated by the key, or similar

❖ CREWEL NEEDLE size 7

❖ EMBROIDERY HOOP

**1 Tracing the design** Use a sharp pencil to trace the ivy design from the following page on to tracing paper. Lay the fabric right side up and position the carbon paper, shiny side down, in one corner. Place the tracing on top so the design lies 9cm (3½in) in from the edges (or 5cm (2in) in on a ready-hemmed cloth). Secure with masking tape or pins on all sides.

**2 Transferring the design** Use a sharp pencil to draw *lightly* over the design lines. Remove the tracing and carbon paper. Transfer the design on to the remaining three corners of the cloth in the same way.

**3 Mounting the fabric in a hoop** Fit the fabric into the hoop, centring the design. If your hoop is not large enough to take the entire design, fit one section and move and remount the fabric as each section is completed.

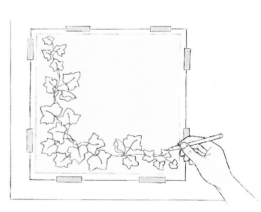

**4 Embroidering the cloth** Follow the key for colours and thread the needle with two strands of embroidery cotton. Taking care to work even stitches and to follow the marked design lines, embroider the leaves in chain stitch and the stems and leaf veins in stem stitch. Move the hoop to work each corner of the cloth in the same way.

---

## ▼▼▼ TIP ▼▼▼

### PROTECTING THE STITCHES

After working each embroidered section remove the hoop and tack a sheet of tissue paper over the embroidery stitches to protect them.

---

**5 Pressing the cloth** When the embroidery is complete, remove the hoop and lay the cloth right side down on a clean, soft towel. With a warm iron, gently press the cloth from the wrong side taking care not to flatten the stitches.

**6 Hemming the edges** Press under a double 2cm (¾in) hem all round the table cloth, forming neat mitred corners. Pin and slipstitch the hem. Using two strands of green, DMC 3347, work a line of chain stitch on the right side just inside the hem.

# MAKING THE NAPKINS

The napkins are made in almost the same way as the table cloth, or you can use ready-made napkins. For an item this small only part of the ivy design is used – in this case the cluster of four leaves at the end of one stalk. However, you can use whichever part of the motif you prefer to create different designs.

**1 Cutting out the napkins**
Using a ruler and set square to ensure that you draw true right angles, mark a 48cm (19in) square on the fabric with tailors' chalk for each napkin. Cut out and press each square.

**2 Marking the design**
Following steps 1 and 2, *Making the Table Cloth*, transfer the four end leaves of the ivy design on to one corner of each napkin, so they lie 5cm (2in) in from the edges (or 3cm (1¼in) on ready-hemmed napkins).

**3 Embroidering the design** Fit the marked corner of one napkin in the embroidery hoop. Using two strands of cotton and following the key for colours, embroider the leaves in chain stitch and the stems and leaf veins in stem stitch. Remove the napkin from the embroidery hoop.

**4 Completing the napkin** Press under a double 1cm (⅜in) hem all round the napkin, mitring the corners. Pin and slipstitch the hem. Following step 6, *Making the Table Cloth*, work a line of chain stitch all round the hem. Embroider and hem each napkin in the same way.

**KEY**

DMC Stranded Embroidery Cotton
2 skeins each of:

368 soft green

471 pale olive green

3347 medium green

1 skein of:

937 dark green

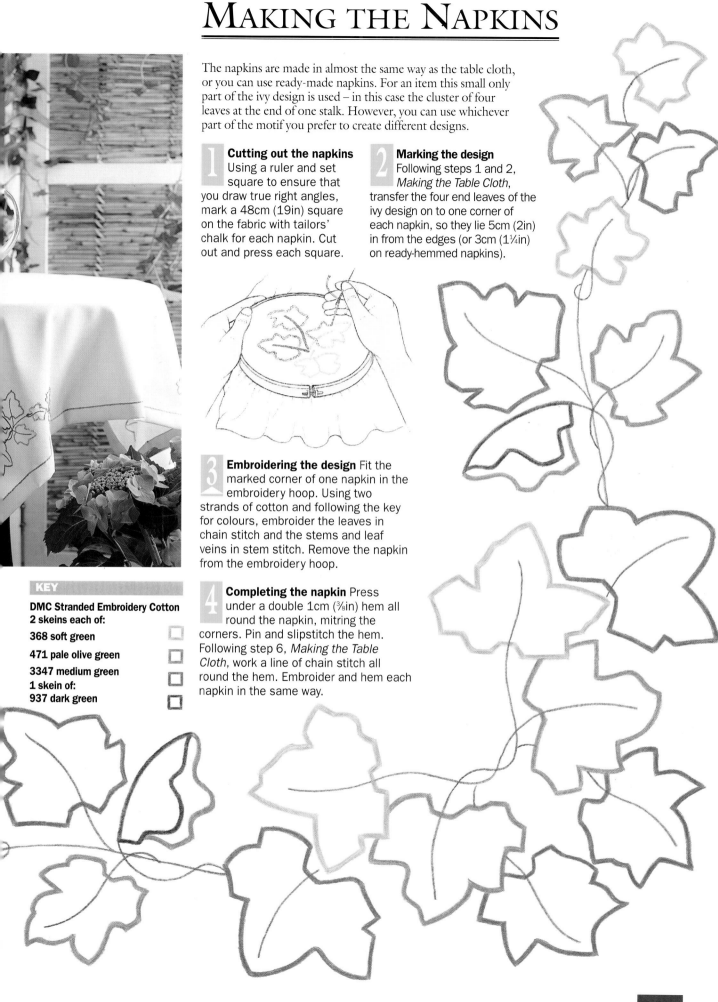

Make these pretty, matching napkin rings from two strips of fabric stiffened with interfacing and stitched into a ring. To neaten the raw edges slipstitch a coordinating colour strip of bias binding, around the outer edge of the ring.

**2 Embroidering the ring** Use an air-erasable pen to mark a line 1.5cm (⅝in) in from both long edges of the main piece of fabric. On the right side of the fabric, work a line of chain stitch along the marked lines using two strands of green DMC stranded embroidery cotton 471.

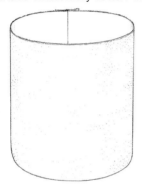

**4 Binding the edges** Fit the lining ring inside the main fabric ring with wrong sides together and matching the raw edges. Cut two pieces of bias binding 18cm (7in) long. Pin one piece of bias binding around each raw edge of the ring, overlapping and tucking under the raw ends. Slipstitch the binding in place around the rings. Make the remaining napkin rings in the same way.

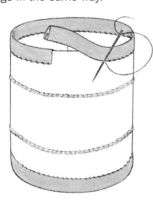

▷ *An embroidered napkin ring, trimmed with a complementary coloured bias binding, ties up the matching set of table linen.*

**1 Cutting the fabric** Use a ruler and set square to draw a rectangle 16 x 10cm (6¼ x 4in) on the fabric. Cut out the rectangle. Fold the rectangle in half lengthways and cut along the fold line. Use one half for the main piece and one half for the lining.

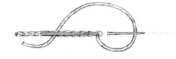

**3 Stitching the rings together** Cut a piece of interfacing the same size as the lining fabric. Fuse the interfacing to the wrong side of the lining fabric following the manufacturer's instructions. With right sides together, fold the lining in half widthways. Matching the raw edges, pin and stitch a 6mm (¼in) seam along the short edge. Press the seam open to form a ring. Fold and stitch the main fabric in the same way.

# Embroidery Stitches

**Embroidery stitches are the building bricks of embroidery design.**

This introduction to embroidery stitches shows how to work a range of the most useful stitches. If you master these basic stitches you will soon be able to work quite complex designs.

Before embarking on a complete embroidered design, try out any stitches you are unfamiliar with on a scrap of embroidery fabric. For worked examples of the stitches below, see over the page.

## Securing Threads

Be sure that the thread is secured with a small backstitch at the beginning and end of your stitching.

To work backstitch, bring the threaded needle from the back to the front of the fabric, leaving a short length of thread loose at the back. Hold the loose end securely and make a small stitch backwards, bringing the needle to the front of the fabric just behind the emerging thread. Take the needle to the back of the fabric again by stitching backwards into the same hole and continue in your chosen embroidery stitch. If possible, work the first embroidery stitch so that it conceals the backstitch.

When you require new thread, change colour or have completed the design, secure with backstitch. Finish with the thread at the back of the fabric.

## Basic chain stitch

One of the most popular embroidery stitches, chain stitch (**A**) is used for outlining or filling in designs. As a filling stitch work in close rows in the same direction, or in a spiral from the centre out.

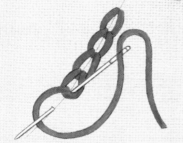

**1 Looping the thread** Bring the needle to the front of the fabric and then insert it back near the same hole. With the thread looped under the point of the needle, bring the needle out a short distance away along the stitching line. Pull stitch through so that the loop lies completely flat.

**2 Working a chain** Repeat along the stitching line, inserting needle back through the hole it has just emerged from for each stitch. Secure the final loop with a small stitch over it into the back of the fabric.

## Lazy daisy (detached chain stitch)

Lazy daisy (**B**) is used as an individual detail, or worked in a circular group to make a flower, with each stitch forming a petal.

**Work separate chain stitches,** starting each stitch at the centre of the flower design and secure each loop with a small stitch. Bring the needle out at the centre of the pattern to start the next stitch.

## Basic backstitch

Backstitch (**C**) is used for outlining or as a baseline for other decorative stitches.

**1 Making the first stitch** Working from right to left, bring the needle to the front of the fabric and take a small stitch backwards. Bring the needle to the front of the fabric ahead of the first stitch, keeping the distance between backward and forward stitches even.

**2 Stitching a line** Create a row of stitches following the pattern line by taking another stitch backwards, inserting the needle through the same hole as the previous stitch.

## Stem stitch

Stem stitch (**D**) is used for outlining or as a decorative pattern for working stems. Worked in close rows it is also used as a filling in stitch.

**1 Forming the stitch** Working from left to right along the line of the design, bring the needle to the front of the fabric. Take a long stitch forwards and, holding the thread to one side of the emerging needle, make a shorter one backwards to the middle of the previous stitch.

## Split stitch

Split stitch (**E**) is worked with stranded cotton and used for outlining, or as solid rows for filling in. It is similar to stem stitch, except when the needle emerges, it splits the thread.

**Working from left to right,** bring needle to the front of the fabric. Take a long stitch forwards and a shorter one backwards, so that the emerging needle splits the thread of the previous stitch. Repeat to stitch a row.

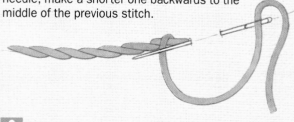

**2 Stitching a row** Repeat the stitch by taking another stitch backwards. Bring the needle out through the same hole as the previous stitch. Keep the stitches even and the thread to the same side of the needle each time.

## Satin stitch

Satin stitch (**F**) is used to create a smooth surface when filling in designs. Work straight parallel lines across the shape of the design so that none of the fabric shows.

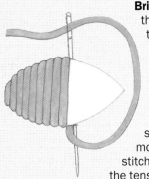

**Bring needle to the front** of the fabric at one edge of the motif and re-insert it on the other side of the motif. Bring needle up again close to where it first emerged and continue making adjacent, parallel stitches to fill in the motif. Do not make stitches too long and keep the tension even or they may pull out of place.

## Slanted satin stitch

Slanted satin stitch (**G**) is worked in the same way as basic satin stitch, with the stitches set at an angle to the motif shape.

**Start the stitches** at the centre of the motif to establish the angle of the slant. Work one half of the design from the centre of the motif out, and then go back to the centre and work the other half of the motif in the opposite direction to fill the motif completely.

# Filling stitches/detached stitches

These stitches are all worked separately. They are used to fill in a design area, creating a bobbly texture, or to form individual decorative features.

## Seeding stitch

Seeding stitch (**H**) is the simplest filler stitch. It can be used singly or in clusters and is often used for shading.

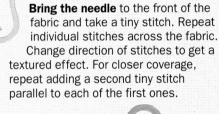

**Bring the needle** to the front of the fabric and take a tiny stitch. Repeat individual stitches across the fabric. Change direction of stitches to get a textured effect. For closer coverage, repeat adding a second tiny stitch parallel to each of the first ones.

## French knots

Small raised stitches, French knots (**I**) add surface interest. When worked close together they give a knobbly texture.

**1 Forming the knot** Bring the needle to the front of the fabric. Holding the thread taut, wrap it twice anti-clockwise round the needle,

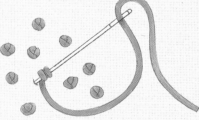

**2 Fixing the knot** Keeping the thread taut, insert the needle back into the fabric, next to the point where it first came through. Pull needle through and secure with backstitch.

## Bullion knots

Bullion knots (**J**) can be used as filling or outlining stitches. Worked in a spiral they form the petals of a rose design.

**1 Winding the thread** Bring needle to the front of the fabric and make a small backstitch. Before drawing the needle fully out of the fabric at the front, wrap the thread five to seven times around it. Pull needle gently through fabric and thread coil, holding the coil flat against the fabric.

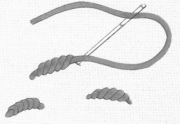

**2 Securing the knot** Pull working thread tight and use point of needle to pack coil threads evenly. Insert needle in the fabric at the end of the coil and work backstitch to secure.

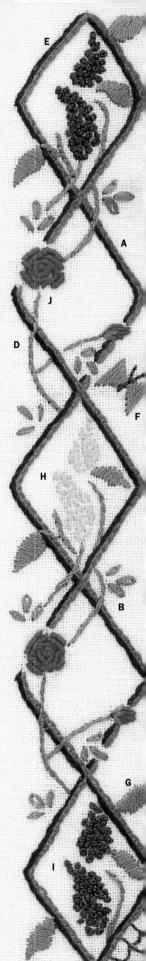

# PIECED CLOTHS

*Piece together household linens such as napkins and tea towels, or some bold bandannas, to create innovative patchwork with a witty design twist – ideal for making throws and tablecloths.*

Next time you fancy embarking on a patchwork project, don't restrict yourself to the classic cotton prints usually favoured; instead, look around the house and through your wardrobe for inspiration. Many household linens, such as tea towels, napkins and lacy runners, or fashion scarves and kerchiefs, can be pieced together to form throws, tablecloths and bedcovers with a difference. And because you're working with large pieces of cloth, the patchwork will be finished in no time.

You can piece together the patchwork cloths in all kinds of ways – in a simple grid format, on the diagonal, or in a more haphazard fashion. Lay them out on the floor to plan the arrangement before you begin stitching. For a well finished look, edge the pieced cloths with a contrasting border, and line them. Decorative top-stitching and trims enhance the effect.

As for any patchwork project, if you mix fabrics make sure they are of a similar weight and have the same care qualities.

*Brightly patterned paisley print bandannas in saffron yellow create a cheery tablecloth for sunny breakfasts and alfresco meals during the summer months – and will give the dinner table a warm glow on dull winter evenings.*

# BANDANNA THROW

This dashing throw is made up from six flaming red cotton bandannas, stitched together then edged and backed with pale blue chambray. You can buy inexpensive bandannas like these in a range of bold colours from department stores and fashion outlets. The throw is interlined for added body, and has white cotton tufts stitched through to hold the fabric layers in place. If you can't find individual tufts, buy a short length of tufted or bobbled braid from a fabric department and trim off the tufts or bobbles. Contrast embroidery – either machine zigzagging or handworked feather stitch – along the throw's border seamline adds a decorative finishing touch.

The finished size of the throw depends on the size of the bandannas. As a guide, the bandannas used here measured 53cm (21in) when trimmed (see step 1 below), giving a finished throw size of 167 x 117cm (65¾ x 46in). Whatever size of bandannas used, they must be square and all the same size.

Hand or machine wash the bandannas separately before making up the throw to check that they are colourfast; if you find the colour runs a lot – often the case with cheap bandannas – you might prefer to dry clean the finished throw.

## YOU WILL NEED

- ❖ SIX BANDANNAS
- ❖ CONTRASTING FABRIC for border and backing
- ❖ COTTON INTERLINING
- ❖ SCISSORS
- ❖ TAPE MEASURE
- ❖ TAILORS' CHALK, PINS
- ❖ MATCHING SEWING THREAD
- ❖ WHITE MACHINE OR HAND EMBROIDERY THREAD
- ❖ SIX WHITE COTTON TUFTS

**1 Preparing the bandannas**
Press the bandannas well. Using a sharp pair of scissors, trim off the hems around each one close to the stitching. Check that the bandannas are all the same size and perfectly square. Adjust if necessary, then neaten the edges with zigzag stitch.

◀ *Flame red bandannas edged with a denim blue chambray border make a dashing throw with a Wild West feel.*

**2 Marking the seamlines** With right sides up, lay the bandannas out in a rectangle, two bandannas wide by three deep. Bearing in mind the bandanna pattern, decide on the depth of the seam allowance – approximately 1.5cm (⅝in). Measure and mark the seam allowance around each bandanna, on the wrong side, using tailors' chalk.

**3 Joining the bandannas** Take the first two bandannas and place them right sides together. Pin and stitch along the marked seamline. Press the seam open. Repeat to stitch the remaining bandannas together into pairs, then stitch the pairs together in the same way to make up the rectangular throw, matching the seamlines exactly.

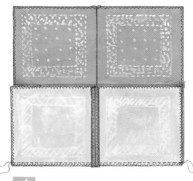

**Adding the border** Cut one set only of 11.5cm (4½in) wide border strips and stitch them in place around the edges of the bandannas.

**5 Embroidering the throw** Cut interlining to the same size as the bandannas plus the border, joining widths if necessary. Pin and tack to the wrong side of the bandannas, matching outer edges. Set your sewing machine to a wide zigzag, and thread with white topstitching thread. Zigzag stitch along the border seamline, on the right side. Alternatively, work feather stitch by hand along border using white embroidery thread.

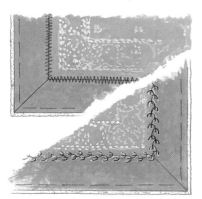

**6 Adding the backing** To back the throw, cut a piece of fabric the same size as the front piece. Place backing on the front, right sides together and the edges matching, and pin and stitch all round, leaving an opening centrally in one short side. Trim the seam allowances and turn right side out. Turn in the opening edges and slipstitch them together. Remove the tacking stitches.

**7 Stitching on the tufts** Hand sew one tuft to the centre of each bandanna, on the right side of the throw, stitching through all layers to anchor the interlining in place. If you wish, you can stitch tufts in corresponding positions on the back of the throw to make this more decorative and conceal the stitches worked through from the front.

▽ *Crisp white and blue tea towels often look far too appealing to be put to their intended use. Give them a more elevated role in your home by piecing them together – some side by side and some overlaid – to form a delightful tablecloth. Conceal and embellish any unsightly seams with toning blue and white braid and ribbon, and edge the cover with a deep blue border.*

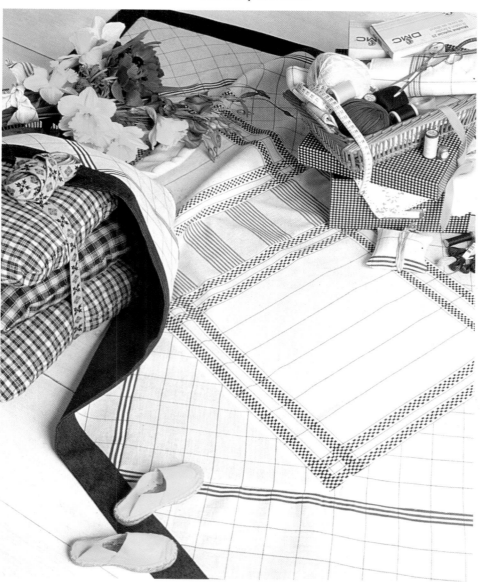

# NAPKIN TOP CLOTH

### YOU WILL NEED

❖ 9 DAMASK NAPKINS
❖ LINEN for borders
❖ WHITE AND ECRU LACE
❖ LACY BRAID
❖ TAPE MEASURE
❖ MATCHING THREAD
❖ FABRIC to back the cloth

Piece together old-fashioned damask napkins to make a classic teatime top cloth. This type of napkin can be used either way up, so you can flip some napkins for a subtle mix and match effect. The napkins are divided by linen border strips, embellished with lace and braid to add prettily textured detailing. You can use any size napkin, but they must all be square and the same size. This cloth is made from napkins trimmed down to 25cm (10in) square to make a top cloth 97cm (39¼in) square. The lace trims are about 3cm (1¼in) wide, and the braid slightly narrower.

**1 Planning the arrangement** Prepare the napkins as for the *Bandanna Throw*, step 1. Lay out the napkins in a three by three format to find an arrangement you like.

**2 Joining the napkins** Measure one napkin and, from linen, cut six strips to this length by 8cm (3¼in) wide. Right sides together and edges matching, join the first three napkins in the arrangement, with a linen band in between, taking a 1cm (⅜in) seam. Repeat to make up two more bands of three napkins. Press the seams open.

**3 Making up the cloth** Measure across one of the bands of three napkins and, from cream linen, cut two strips to this length by 8cm (3¼in) wide. Join together the bands of napkins, inserting a linen strip between them, as in step 2.

**4 Decorating the cloth** Cut two lengths of ecru lace and two of white lace, to the current width of the top cloth. Lay the two ecru lace lengths centrally along the border strips dividing the linen squares in one direction, and pin and topstitch in place. Repeat to stitch the white lace lengths centrally along the border strips in the other direction.

**5 Adding the border** Following step 4 of the *Bandanna Throw*, cut 10cm (4in) wide border strips from white linen and stitch in place around the napkins. Cut ecru lace and lacy braid to fit all round the border plus a little extra for turnings. Pin and topstitch the lace centrally round the border, on the right side, neatly mitring the corners and turning under the raw ends. Repeat to stitch the braid centrally over the lace. Line the cloth as for the *Bandanna Throw*, step 6.

▼ *Traditional damask napkins in subtle tones of cream and beige are teamed with linen and lace to make a charming top cloth.*

# FABRIC PLACE MATS

*You can create the most elegant of place settings with simple octagonal place mats and matching napkins. Trim them with vivid bands of petersham ribbon in colours to complement your tableware.*

S ewing a set of matching fabric mats and napkins is something you can do in an evening, and it needn't cost the earth. A set of four mats and napkins takes little more than a metre and a half (1⅝ yards) of fabric. Line the mats in a toning lining fabric or, for extra versatility, choose an attractive backing fabric so the mats are reversible for a completely different look. Many tables need protection from scorching so add a layer of curtain interlining or thermal lining between the fabric and lining.

It is important to choose washable, shrinkproof fabrics. Accidental spills are a

perennial problem at meal times and a set of mats that you can wash, press and return to the table quickly is very useful. Check that the ribbon trim is also washable and shrinkproof.

Bypass the conventional rectangular form by cutting away the corners to create a more interesting octagonal shape. Petersham ribbon criss-crossing from corner to corner helps to define the shape. Use any spare fabric to make the napkins, then tie them up in rolls with a short length of the same ribbon. Cut the ribbon ends diagonally to prevent fraying and knot them as you would a necktie.

*A designer look is achieved with these quick-to-make place mats. Matching napkins complete the inviting setting.*

99

# MAKING A PLACE MAT AND NAPKIN SET

You make the place mats from layers of ribbon-trimmed fabric, protective interlining and lining, sandwiched and sewn together. Lining the mats gives extra body and ensures that all the raw edges that might fray are hidden inside the mat; interlining ensures your table gets proper protection from hot plates.

Make sure all the fabrics and ribbons you use aren't prone to shrinking when washed and use a washable interlining such as domette for padding. Washable, iron-on wadding is another good choice for interlining. Even for the narrowest width fabric, a set of mats and napkins only takes 1.8m (1⅞yd) of fabric.

## YOU WILL NEED

*For 4 place mats*

❖ PAPER FOR PATTERN

❖ RULER

❖ 80cm (⅞yd) FABRIC

❖ LINING

❖ 80cm (⅞yd) INTERLINING

❖ 8m (8¾yd) of 15mm (⅝in) wide PETERSHAM RIBBON

❖ MATCHING THREAD

*For 4 napkins*

❖ 1m (1yd) FABRIC

❖ 2m (2yd) of 15mm (⅝in) wide PETERSHAM RIBBON

**Making the pattern** On a sheet of paper draw a rectangle 45 x 36cm (18 x 14in). Measure and mark 8cm (3¼in) along the sides from each corner point. Join the marks diagonally across the corners. Cut off the corners and discard them.

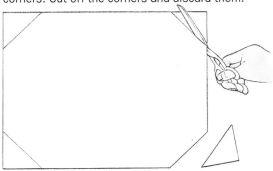

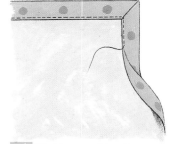

▲ *Team bright table mats with matching napkins tied into a roll with a ribbon bow. For a special look, tuck a few fresh flowers under the bow.*

**Cutting out** Use the pattern to cut out four fabric pieces and four lining pieces, adding 1.5cm (⅝in) all round for seam allowances. Using the pattern, cut the four pieces of interlining, omitting the seam allowance. Position interlining centrally on the wrong side of the fabric and pin and tack (or iron) in place.

**Attaching ribbon** Lay the fabric/interlining right side up. Cut two 39cm (15¼in) lengths of ribbon and position them across the short sides of the fabric, 1.5cm (⅝in) in from corner edges. Pin and topstitch down both sides of ribbon close to edge. Cut two 48cm (19¼in) lengths of ribbon and topstitch across the long sides of the fabric from corner to corner.

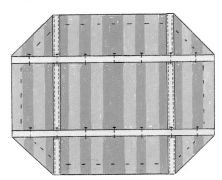

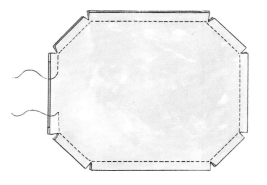

**Adding the lining** With right sides together, pin lining to fabric. Stitch a 1.5cm (⅝in) seam all round, leaving a 10cm (4in) opening in the middle of one side. Clip into the seam allowance at the corners. Turn the mat right side out and press. Turn in the opening edges and slipstitch to close.

**Making napkins** For each napkin cut a 44cm (17¼in) square. Turn under and press a double 1cm (⅜in) hem, forming neat mitres at each corner. Pin and topstitch 6mm (¼in) from hem edge, all round napkin. Cut a 50cm (20in) length of ribbon diagonally to tie up each napkin.

# Guide to Ribbons

## Discover the tempting range of ribbons available for use in home furnishing projects.

Ribbons are one of the quickest and most inexpensive ways to brighten up household furnishings and accessories. They come in a superb range of colours, textures and patterns, including themed designs, so you are sure to find one that's just right for the project in hand. This useful guide takes you through the most widely available types of ribbon. The most popular kinds (single and double-faced satin ribbon) come in an extensive variety of widths, from 1.5-75mm (¹⁄₁₆-3in), while more unusual designs, such as jacquard, have a more limited size range.

**Single-faced satin ribbon** This ribbon has one shiny and one matt side, and is the most commonly used. It can be stitched on to soft furnishings, woven through eyelet lace and glued on to a range of surfaces. Single-faced ribbons come in a good selection of plain colours, self-patterns, such as polka dots, and printed patterns. Widths range from 1.5-75mm (¹⁄₁₆-3in).

**Double-faced satin ribbon** This satin ribbon is shiny on both sides and slightly thicker than *single-faced satin ribbon*. It is available in a wide range of plain colours and widths. Use it for applications where both sides of the ribbon will be visible – for example, ribbon ties, bows and roses. This ribbon is available in a wide range of widths from extra-fine 1.5mm (¹⁄₁₆in) to 75mm (3in).

**Picot ribbon** Picot ribbons have a pretty looped border along one or both edges. You can buy plain satin, petersham and other more decorative ribbons with picot edges.

**Crêpe ribbon** This ribbon has the texture of crêpe paper or fabric, and a lustrous finish. It is available in a range of plain colours, in silk or polyester.

**Taffeta ribbon** This is a crisp, firm ribbon with a matt finish, ideal for creating sharp bows. Taffeta ribbon is available plain or checked in many colours and widths and also with a water-marked finish, such as moiré.

**Sheer ribbon** This is a light, semi-transparent ribbon which may be printed or plain, sometimes with a silky sheen. Some sheer ribbons are finished with a decorative satin edge or with lengthways satin stripes. Use sheer ribbon to hold back sheer curtains with lavish bows or to make fragile ribbon roses or rosettes.

**Grosgrain** A strong, firm ribbon with a distinctive crossways rib. Grosgrain comes in a variety of plain colours as well as in printed lengthways stripes.

**Velvet ribbon** (see overleaf) Velvet ribbon has a soft, raised pile and may be nylon or cotton. It is available as a single or double-faced ribbon and in a good range of deep rich colours as well as some pastel shades. Velvet tube ribbon is also available.

single-faced satin

double-faced satin

picot

silk crêpe

polyester crêpe

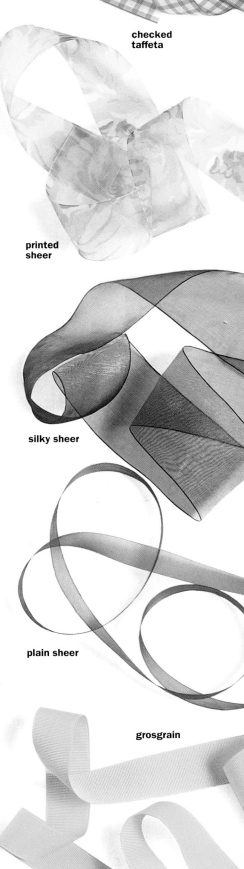

checked taffeta

printed sheer

silky sheer

plain sheer

grosgrain

**Printed ribbon** This has a pattern printed on one side. Some novelty printed ribbons are designed for special occasions, such as Christmas or weddings, or they have designs suitable for children.

**Jacquard ribbon** Woven in a similar style to the fabric of the same name, these ribbons have a slightly raised often floral design. On the wrong side the different coloured yarns run along the ribbon between colours and patterns. Jacquard ribbon is sometimes woven with metallic threads for a more striking effect.

**Tartan ribbon** Increasingly popular, tartan ribbon comes in a wide variety of designs – from authentic clan tartans to fantasy checks. The ribbon may be satin, taffeta or petersham, and the design either woven or printed.

**Pre-pleated ribbon** Pre-pleated ribbon has knife, concertina or box pleats. Use it as a decorative edging on cushions and curtains.

**Wire-edged ribbon** This has a fine wire woven along the edges, so you can twist and mould it into loops, waves and folds and it will hold its shape. You can buy it in sheer to mediumweight fabrics and in several widths and designs. Use wire-edged ribbon to create sculptured picture bows and rosettes.

**Petersham** This is extra strong ribbon with a pronounced crossways rib. Available in a good range of colours and widths, petersham can be used to decorate many items in the home, including heavy brocade cushions and hat and shoe boxes.

**Pre-gathered ribbon** A gathering thread runs along one edge of this ribbon. Pull the thread right up to create quick ribbon rosettes, or use the ribbon as a frilled trim for cushions. Pre-gathered ribbon is available in a range of plain colours and printed designs.

**Embellished ribbon** Embellished ribbons have beads and/or sequins sewn on to a plain satin surface – ideal for putting on the glitz.

**Metallic ribbon** Woven from lurex and similar metallic fibres, metallic ribbon comes in a variety of finishes from sheer to crossways ribbed effects. It's perfect for adding sparkle to festive accessories and decorations, and for tying up special gifts.

**Craft ribbon** Also known as florists' ribbon, this consists of a thin strip of fabric, coated with a finish so the edges will not fray when cut. Unwashable, the ribbons are best used for craft projects rather than sewing. They are available in a wide range of plain colours and a variety of distinctive patterns.

**Paper ribbon** This is available in two forms – as a flat, textured ribbon stored on spools, or as a tightly twisted ribbon which, when unwound, gives a decorative crinkled effect. You can use it for many craft projects.

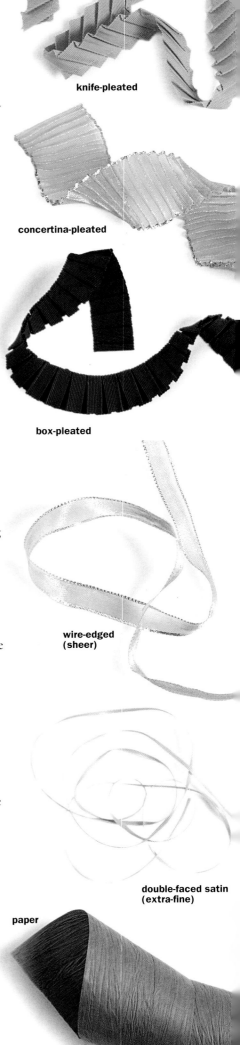

single-faced velvet

printed child's ribbon

jacquard

tartan

knife-pleated

concertina-pleated

box-pleated

wire-edged (sheer)

double-faced satin (extra-fine)

paper

# Working with Ribbons

**You can use ribbons in many ways to add decorative detail to your soft furnishings.**

From straightforward appliqué to more flamboyant pleated, gathered or zigzag edgings, ribbon trims have a strong decorative role to play on household furnishings such as lampshades, cushions, bedlinen and tiebacks. Their non-fray edges make them easy to work with, giving quick results. The majority of ribbons are made from synthetic fibres, so they're colourfast and unlikely to shrink – a bonus if you want to machine wash your furnishings; however, there are exceptions, so if in doubt always test-wash a sample.

## Ribbon appliqué

Ribbons are ideal for machine appliqué because they have pre-finished side edges and so can simply be topstitched in place. For a neat finish, match the machine bobbin thread to the background fabric and the needle thread to the ribbon, or choose a contrast colour. Always tuck under the short ends of the ribbon, unless they will be stitched into a seam. On medium and wide ribbons, be sure to stitch in the same direction down both sides to prevent puckering. Tack the ribbons in place first.

### Narrow ribbon
Couch narrow ribbon in place by working over it with zigzag stitch, using either a thread to match the ribbon or a contrasting colour.

### Medium and wide ribbon
Use straight stitch and matching or contrasting thread to stitch down both side edges of the ribbon, just inside the ridged edges. Alternatively, zigzag stitch over the ribbon edges for a more decorative effect.

### Appliqué edgings
This technique gives a decorative finish if you want to appliqué ribbon edgings on to the fabric surface, rather than enclosing them in a seam. Secure the ribbon trim on the fabric and lay a length of medium-width ribbon along its top edge. Topstitch in place along all edges, catching in the trim.

## Gathering ribbon

Gathered ribbons are a quick way to add soft frills to furnishings. You can gather along one edge and insert the frill in a seam, or gather down the middle to create a ruche for surface appliqué. Try layering up two lengths of ribbon to create double frills.

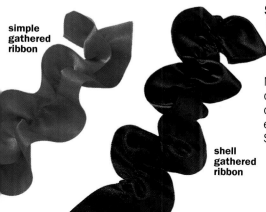

**simple gathered ribbon**

**shell gathered ribbon**

### Simple gathered ribbon
Work the gathering by machine for quick results. Loosen the tension slightly on your sewing machine and set it to a long stitch length. Machine stitch a single row of stitches down the centre of the ribbon or along one edge. Pull up the bobbin thread evenly to gather up the ribbon gently. Secure the thread ends.

### Shell gathered ribbon
Mark at 2.5-5cm (1-2in) intervals down each side of the ribbon with tailors' chalk. Use a needle and thread and running stitch, or long machine stitches, to stitch in a zigzag line down the length of the ribbon, working between alternate marks on each edge. Carefully pull up the gathering thread, forming shell-like shapes. Fasten off the thread end(s).

103

# Pleating ribbon

Though you can buy pre-pleated ribbons, the colour and pattern range is limited, so pleating your own is a useful skill. Crisp ribbons, such as grosgrain and taffeta, hold their shape particularly well when pleated and are the easiest to work with.

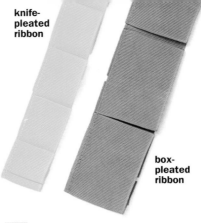

knife-pleated ribbon

box-pleated ribbon

## Knife-pleated ribbon
Multiply the desired finished length of the pleated trim by three to find how much ribbon you need.

**1 Making a template** To make a template, cut a rectangular piece of card twice the ribbon width, by the desired finished width of each pleat.

**2 Pinning the pleats** Lay the ribbon out flat. Lay the template over the ribbon at one end, lining up the side edge with the ribbon's short end. Fold the ribbon across the template and back again to form a pleat. Finger press, carefully slip out the template and pin the pleat in place. Repeat all along the ribbon with the pleats lying side by side.

## Box-pleated ribbon
Calculate ribbon quantities as for the *Knife-pleated ribbon* above.

**1 Making a template** Cut a rectangular card template twice the ribbon width, by the desired finished width of each pleat. Draw a line down the centre.

**2 Pinning the pleats** Lay the template, marked side up, over the ribbon at one end, and fold in the ribbon on each side to meet the marked line. Finger press, then slip out the template and pin the pleat in place. Repeat all along the ribbon, leaving no spaces between pleats.

**3 Stitching the pleats** Machine stitch the pleats in place, either along one edge or down the centre, removing the pins as you go.

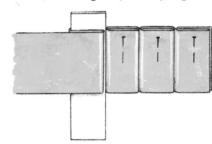

**3 Stitching the pleats** Machine stitch the pleats along one edge or down the centre, removing pins as you go.

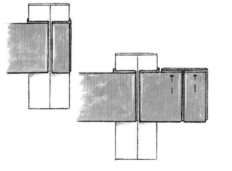

## Box-pleated ruche
Box-pleat the ribbon as described below left, securing the pleats by stitching down the *middle* of the ribbon. Pinch together the opposite sides of each box pleat and secure with a few hand stitches across the centre of the upper edge. If you wish, you can add a tiny bead at each point, or stitch using a range of contrast threads.

box-pleated ruche

---

# Zigzag edgings

You can fold ribbons to create decorative zigzag edgings – an original alternative to the pleated styles above. Use a double-sided ribbon as both sides will show clearly.

## Triangular edging
Cut the ribbon into short lengths 5-7.5cm (2-3in) long depending on the desired finished depth of the edging. On one length, turn in both ends to meet at the base, forming a triangular shape. Pin the ends of the ribbon triangle in place on the right side of the fabric, so they will be caught in the seam. Repeat to fold and attach more triangles, placing them side by side or at intervals. Stitch the seam, catching in the base of each triangle.

## Open edging
Lay the ribbon in regular zigzag folds across the right side of the fabric, lining up the base edge with the fabric raw edge. Pin the ribbon in place, then stitch the seam, catching in the ribbon.

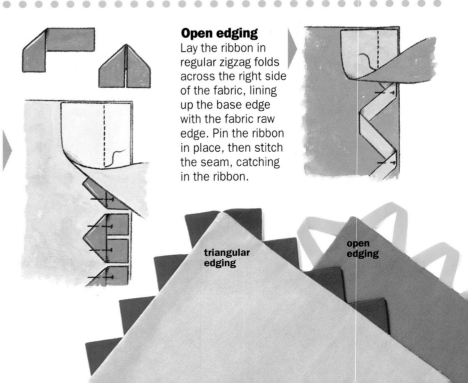

triangular edging

open edging

# Rosettes

**Add decorative touches to soft furnishings with rosettes made from pleated or ruched fabric.**

Whether used as fine detailing for tiebacks, swags and tails or for pelmets and bed canopies, fabric rosettes are most effective for highlighting significant features in the room. You can also use them in a more practical way to disguise joins in the fabric or unsightly gathers and fixtures.

You can make any of the following rosettes quickly, without needing any specialist tools or skills. They look good in a variety of mix and match fabrics, so they're a good opportunity for using up oddments of attractive fabric. You can also let your imagination run wild with dashes of highly decorative fabrics, in a shocking colour or with a metallic effect, for example.

## Pleated rosettes

These are the most elegant and formal of the rosettes, with a circle of fabric sharply pleated round a central button. Use crisp cotton or silk furnishing fabrics for crisp pleats. Cover the button in a matching or contrasting fabric. You can make pleated rosettes from a strip of fabric folded in half or a single strip of a more textured fabric with the raw outer edges bound with cotton or satin bias binding. Choose a toning or contrasting binding and cover the central button to match.

**1 Checking the size** Decide on the finished diameter of the rosette and draw a circle to match on a sheet of paper. Measure round the circumference of the marked circle and cut a strip of fabric three times this length by the finished diameter of the rosette. Cut a circle of fabric for covering the button.

**2 Preparing the fabric** With right sides together, fold the fabric strip in half lengthways. Pin and stitch across both ends, taking a 1cm (⅜in) seam allowance. Trim across the corners and turn right side out. Press the strip with seams to edge. Neaten and join the raw edges together with a row of straight or zigzag stitching.

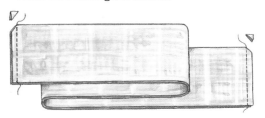

**3 Marking out the pleats** Place pins vertically into the folded edge at 2.5cm (1in) intervals. If you want larger pleats, increase the distance between the pins slightly. Even out the pleat size so there is an even number of pleats along the strip.

---

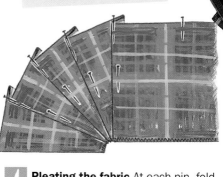

**4 Pleating the fabric** At each pin, fold the fabric into even pleats, working round in a curve. At the centre, overlap the edges for each pleat so that only a small amount of fabric is visible. Finger press and pin pleats as you work.

**5 Stitching the pleats** When you have finished pleating the whole strip, tuck the end of the strip under the first pleat and pin. Even out the pleats round the rosette as necessary. Using a double thread, hand stitch the pleats at the centre to hold them in place.

**6 Neatening the centre** Following the manufacturer's instructions, cover the button with fabric. Stitch the button in position in the middle of the rosette.

## PLEATED RIBBON ROSETTES

For shortcut rosettes, you can use plain or patterned ribbons arranged round a felt disc. You need 1.30m (1⅓yd) of 25mm (1in) wide ribbon for 10cm (4in) rosette.

Cut the ribbon into fourteen 9cm (3½in) lengths. Cut out a 6.5cm (2½in) diameter circle of felt as the base. Press each piece of ribbon in half widthways. Fan out the folded ribbons evenly from the centre of the felt as shown.

Stitch the ribbons together in the centre through the felt. Cover the centre with a covered button as in *Pleated Rosettes*.

# Maltese cross rosette

This rosette is a simple alternative to the pleated rosette. Depending on how elaborate you want the cross effect to be, the rosette is made by laying two or three bows on top of each other and holding them together with a covered button.

The bows are formed from a loop of doubled fabric or a single strip of fabric with bound raw edges, gathered up in the centre. Use crisp furnishing cotton for the doubled strip and a slightly heavier fabric when binding the edges.

**2 Stitching each loop** Fold each loop in half lengthways with right sides together. Pin and stitch the long raw edges together. Turn right side out. Centre the seam along the back and press the strip flat. Make up each loop in the same way. Alternatively, pin and stitch bias binding along both long raw edges. Neaten both ends with zigzag stitch.

**3 Creating the bows** With seam on the inside, turn in raw edges of first piece so they overlap slightly in the centre. Work two rows of gathering stitches down the centre through all layers. Pull up gathers to create a bow shape on either side of centre; fasten off gathering thread.

**4 Making up a simple cross** Matching centres, place two loops at right angles to each other. Hand stitch through the centre to hold all layers together. Cover a button and sew in centre of loops.

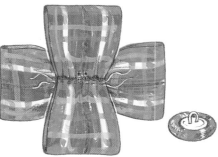

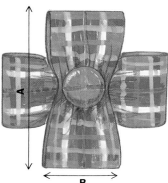

**1 Cutting the fabric** Decide on the finished size (**A**) and cut two or three strips of fabric (depending on the effect you want) twice the finished diameter of the rosette by twice the finished width of each loop (**B**). Add 1cm (⅜in) seam allowance all round each piece and cut out. Cut a circle of fabric for covering the button.

## DOUBLE ROSETTES

Layering rosettes together creates a design flourish. Decide on the finished diameter of the multiple rosette and make up one rosette to that size. Then make a second one, 2cm (¾in) in diameter smaller than the first, and a third 2cm (¾in) smaller than that. Place the rosettes one on top of the other in decreasing size and hand stitch them together in the centre. Cover the raw edges with a button as before.

# Puff-ball rosette

This gathered ball of fabric makes a scrunchy rosette which works as well in a glamorous bedroom as it does in a plainer setting. Choose lightweight sheer or glossy fabrics such as moiré or silk to emphasize the folds.

**1 Cutting the fabric** Decide on the finished size of the rosette and cut a circle of fabric two to three times the required diameter. The larger the circle compared to the finished size, the more scrunched the finished rosette looks.

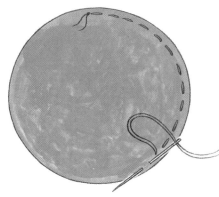

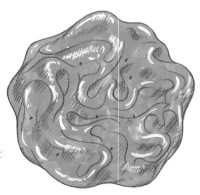

**2 Gathering up the rosette** Thread a needle with button thread and knot the ends together to make a double thread. Work a row of gathering stitches round the circumference of the circle, 1.5cm (⅝in) from the edge, leaving the thread ends on the right side. Pull up the gathers to form a small circle and fasten off the thread.

**3 Creating the puff ball** Using matching thread, take a small stitch through the centre of the circle. Then, working from the right side, scrunch up the fabric with one hand and take small stitches in the hollows about halfway between the outer edge and the centre. Work further stitches until a well-rounded shape is achieved; fasten off the thread.

# BRAID ABOUNDS

*Opulent braids, fanciful fringing or simple twists of cord bring out the best in soft furnishings and accessories – whether they're defining the edge of a cushion or adding pizzazz to a picture frame.*

P assementerie, the craft of making elaborate braids, tassels, cords and fringing, is flourishing and supplying a tantalizing selection of exciting trims to fabric departments. From inexpensive, single twist cords to lavish and costly woven braids, there are trims in any desired colour to suit every scheme and all budgets. With a little invention, you can use braids, fringing and tassels to add energy and an individual twist to the plainest or most polished of decorative items.

Most braids are stitched on by hand, so you'll have no trouble adding them to existing items, and in some cases you can even glue

them in place. So, look round your home for any items that would benefit from a little trimming. There's no need to limit your ideas to traditional furnishings – trims are useful in all sorts of unexpected and exciting ways.

Try out novel ideas such as gluing braid along the edge of shelves, table tops or even in place of a wallpaper border or along the top of a chair rail. Wrap remnants of a favourite braid round everyday items such as glass vases or plain candlesticks, to add interest and texture; or treat yourself to a luxurious braid to cheer up tired curtains or to give cushion covers and upholstery a new lease of life.

*Unexpected treasures result when you add braid to basic household objects. Sticking scraps of your favourite braids to photograph frames or glass vases with all-purpose adhesive immediately links these items to the other decorations in your home; on the vase, the braids hide the flower stems as well.*

◀ **Opulent gold fringing** repeats and reinforces the richness of the fabrics used to make these eyecatching cushion covers and adds a dancing edge.

◣ **Dress up understated tablelamps** with fringing or braid. Coiled, narrow braid disguises the entire base of one lamp, while fringing adds a whimsical touch to the shade. A patterned braid adds interest to the base of the second lamp.

◣ **With a touch of impromptu flair**, Aztec-inspired braid jazzes up table accessories for an informal, festive meal. Trim napkins with wildly bright braid for an equally bold flourish.

▶ **Handsome yellow and blue braid**, stitched down the leading edges, lightens the look of heavy navy curtains and links them to the lively hues of the sofa upholstery. Coordinating blue and yellow twisted cord tiebacks are another unifying touch.

# TASSEL MAGIC

*Tassels are high fashion and great fun –*
*fix them to soft furnishings and accessories around the home*
*for all sorts of stylish finishing flourishes.*

T he beauty of tassels is that they are so ver-satile – you can use them almost anywhere to trim just about anything. As well as using them conventionally on soft furnish-ings such as curtains and cushions, attach tas-sels to all sorts of accessories around the home – lampshades, pictures and mirrors, for exam-ple, can all be made to look extra special with a tassel trim.

Whatever the colour and style of your fur-nishings, well chosen tassels can enhance their look. Tassels both transform the plain and embellish the opulent. Wherever you use them they add a touch of colour and class.

Tassels and tasselled braids and cords come in almost every colour and style imaginable. You are spoilt for choice – so give free rein to your creative talents, and experiment with dif-ferent ideas all around the home.

For an interesting effect, don't duplicate colours and patterns precisely; aim for a bold contrast, or go instead for a subtler, complementary match. Either way you are making your furnishings more interesting and introducing fresh, new colours into the room.

*Silky*
*and richly coloured*
*tassels and tasselled braid give*
*these covered hat boxes a*
*flamboyant yet elegant trim.*

◱ **Thick, chunky tassels** *and a simple fringe in rich raspberry red make a bold statement in complementing the curtain and pelmet while adding texture and depth.*

◩ **Tying tasselled cord** *around fabric wrapped cushions and bolsters produces an instant and amusing effect.*

◮ **Generous fringing** *sweeps down to link one tasselled cord hanging from the rail with another holding back the curtain.*

◮ **Perfect match** – *the tasselled cord goes so well with the flowers and frame that they could have been made for each other.*

# Tassel Making Guide

**Making your own tassels is both rewarding and cost-effective.**

There is a wide selection of ready-made tassels available, ranging from quite inexpensive examples to very costly ones, heavily embellished with silken braids, cords and other adornments. The advantage of making your own is that you can tailor them to suit your own decor and, in the case of the larger, more expensive tassels, save some money into the bargain. While you can buy the special tools and moulds used by professionals for making tassels, it is possible to improvise using readily-available materials that you can adapt for the purpose. There is an inexhaustible range of threads, yarns, ready-made fringing, cords, beads and baubles that you can use.

## Materials and equipment

**Adhesive** You can use adhesive to stick together ready-made trimmings when making tassels.

**Cardboard** (1) Firm cardboard, trimmed to different widths, is a useful form round which to wind yarns to make the tassel tails. Alternatively, you could use a book or other firm, flat object.

**Couronne sticks** (2) These are special sticks of turned wood used for winding loops of yarn. They are graduated to allow you to wind loops of different circumferences.

**Crochet hook** (3) Use a crochet hook for looping yarn through large beads.

**Moulds** One way of making the head of a tassel is to wrap yarn round a mould. *Traditional tassel moulds* (4) are made from wood and are available from specialist suppliers, but you can use any suitably sized form with a central hole. *Polystyrene* or *paper craft balls* (5), a *large bead* (6), a *cotton reel* (7), *curtain rings* and even a *plastic light fitting* are all suitable.

**Needles** (8) When covering a tassel mould it is easiest to use a *tapestry* or *wool darning needle*, with an eye large enough to take the yarn you have chosen.

**Ornaments** B*eads* (9) and *trinkets* (10) add interest to tassels. Attach small beads to the tail threads and place larger beads at the neck of the tassel.

**Trimmings** Ready-made trimmings are useful for making instant tassels. Roll up *bullion* (11) or *cut fringe* (12) and then stitch or glue it together to make a tassel tail. Coil *braid* (13) or *cord* (14) around the top of the tail to make the head.

**Yarn** Unless you are using ready-made trimmings you need yarn for most aspects of tassel making. Almost any type of yarn is suitable: *knitting or tapestry wool* (15), *string, embroidery cotton* (16) and *metallic thread* (17), *leather thongs* (18), *chenille* (19) or *fine ribbons* (20) are excellent examples. To avoid a messy finish, try to choose yarns that do not fray. Also consider the scale of the tassel you are making and choose the thickness of yarn accordingly – a thicker yarn twists into a wider cord, makes a bulkier tassel tail and covers a tassel mould more quickly than a fine yarn.

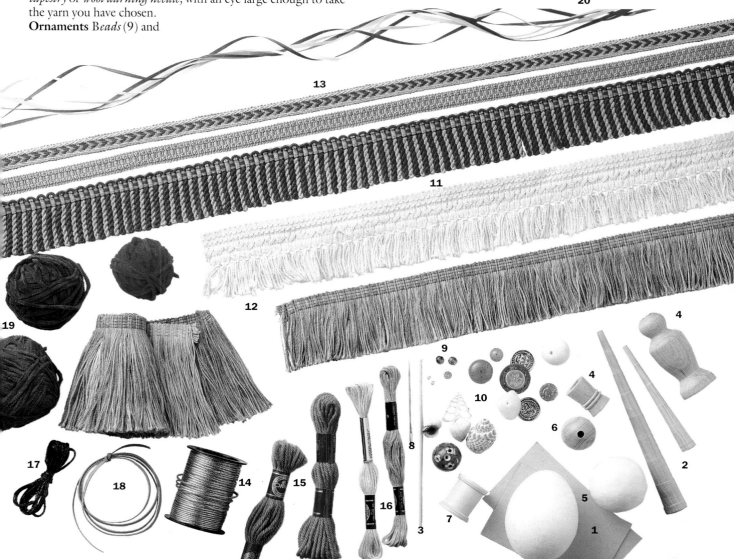

# Working with yarn

When you're making tassels, it is important to keep your chosen yarns organized, or you may end up in a tremendous tangle. If you are using skeins or balls of embroidery or knitting yarn to make the tassel, it is simpler to wind the yarn on to pieces of card first. For added speed and when you're using a mixture of different colours, wind lengths of yarn on to the card together and treat them as one when you unravel them.

**Preparing mixed yarns** Take the end from each skein or ball of yarn. Place the ends of the yarns together. Wind the yarns simultaneously around a piece of card or a book. When using the yarns unravel them as one strand.

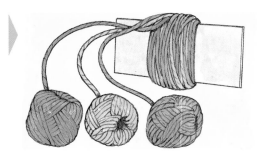

## Foldover tassels

Foldover tassels are very simple to make using any type of yarn. Make them to any length and thickness depending on the size of item you are trimming. You can use them on their own to trim cushions or other small items of soft furnishing, to make a fringed trim or to add interest to a larger tassel.

**1 Winding the yarn** Cut a piece of stiff card the required length of the tassel, or use a book this size. With the ends at the bottom edge, wrap yarn evenly around the card to the thickness you want.

**2 Taking the loops off the form** Thread a needle with some of the yarn. Insert the needle under the loops and tie them loosely together. Ease the loops off the card.

**3 Tying the tassel** Cut a length of yarn about 80cm (32in) long. Wrap it around the tassel about one-third down from the top of the loops and secure it with a knot. Continue wrapping the yarn around the tassel, covering the knot. Thread the loose end on to a tapestry needle and stitch it into the centre of the tassel, down into the tail. Cut and trim the loops at the bottom of the tassel.

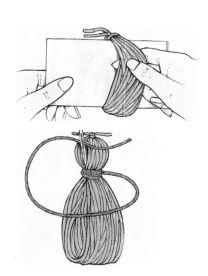

## Twisted cord

Cord consists of one or more lengths of yarn twisted together. Use it to make the rope for a tassel-trimmed tieback, as an edging trim for cushions, or as part of a tassel, perhaps holding smaller tassels or beads. You can make cord with most types of yarn. Use thin yarn for fine cord, and thick yarn for chunky cord – or just vary the number of strands accordingly. Experiment with short lengths of your chosen yarn to find the number of strands needed to achieve the desired thickness. As you must hold both ends of the threads as you twist them, it is easier if you have someone to help you twist very long cords.

**2 Making the cord** Fold the twisted yarns in half and tie the two ends together. Allow the folded end to drop down, then shake out the cord so the strands twist around each other. Run your hand a few times down the cord to even out the twists.

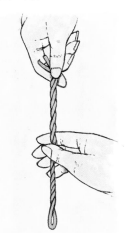

### Making a one-colour cord

**1 Preparing the yarn** Cut the yarn into the required number of lengths, two and a half times the desired length of the completed cord. Match the yarn ends and, holding an end in each hand, pull the yarns taut. Then twist each end clockwise at the same time until the yarn is tightly twisted.

### Making a two-colour cord

Cut the yarn into the required number of lengths in each colour, with each length one and a half times the desired completed length of the cord. Keeping the different colours separate, knot them together at one end. Hold the ends of the different colours apart, so the knot is positioned halfway along the yarns. Twist the yarns together and finish the cord as for *Making a one-colour cord*.

# STENCILLING ON FABRIC

*Knowing how to stencil fabric opens up many possibilities for decorating your home, from improving the look of inexpensive, plain fabrics to creating a completely coordinated scheme throughout a room.*

The techniques for stencilling fabric are much the same as those for stencilling on wood or walls. Paint is applied using a brush or sponge through the cut-out areas of a stencil to create a design motif. By repeating the motif you can produce borders or patterns.

Stencilling adds charm to plain or inexpensive fabrics, and is an economical way of decorating a room. You can either stencil lengths of fabric with original designs for making up your own soft furnishings, or you can stencil ready-made items such as a cushion or lampshade.

If you feel that the existing decor needs a lift, a stencil is a good solution. Pre-cut stencils are available in different designs, so you should be able to find one to tie in with other patterns in the room. You can then use your chosen design to decorate walls, furniture and other accessories for a uniquely coordinated scheme.

*Bold moon and star motifs are ideal for a child's bedroom. Here a selection of stencils on the same theme are used on curtains and accessories to give an attractive coordinated look.*

# CHOOSING MATERIALS

You can buy pre-cut stencils from do-it-yourself stores and craft shops. Some manufacturers produce stencils to match their coordinated ranges, so you can stencil the fabric for a pair of curtains to echo the theme on a wallpaper or border from the range.

### SUITABLE FABRICS

The fibre content of the fabric you are stencilling is important. Natural fibres, such as cotton and linen, or fabrics containing a large proportion of cotton, take paint well. You also get a more clearly defined stencilled motif on a fabric with a smooth weave than a textured one. When buying fabrics, consider inexpensive choices such as calico or plain cottons – they look just as effective as more costly cloths.

### PREPARING THE FABRIC

Before you start, wash the item or fabric to remove any manufacturers' finishes. You can, however, stencil items such as roller blinds or lampshades that you cannot pre-wash without any treatment.

For the best results, stretch the fabric taut before stencilling. You can improvise by stretching small items over a board or embroidery frame while larger items, such as curtains, need to be stretched out on a table. Stiff fabrics, in roller blinds for example, are firm enough without being held taut – just weight them down with heavy objects at the corners to prevent them from slipping while you stencil.

### CHOOSING PAINTS

Water-based fabric paints are ideal, as they dry leaving the surface of the fabric soft and pliable. They are available from craft and art shops, by mail order and from do-it-yourself stores in a wide range of colours and different finishes, including pearlized, opaque and transparent effects. For fabrics that don't require regular washing, artists' acrylics, car spray paints or household emulsion are all suitable. It is worth testing these paints on a scrap of fabric, because they may dry stiff and inflexible, which spoils the draping quality of the finished fabric.

### PRACTISE FIRST

Once applied to the fabric, paint marks become permanent or are difficult to remove. To avoid mistakes, practise on a sample of the fabric to see how the paint behaves and how much you need to use to get the desired effect. It's a good idea to start with a small item such as a cushion cover as a first project.

The colour of the fabric affects the colour of the paint. For clear colours you need to work on a pale or neutral fabric and use opaque paints. You can use dark fabrics, but the paint shade is more likely to be altered, especially if the paint is translucent. When stencilling darker fabrics with a pale colour, such as the white on the blue fabric shown here, stencil over the area twice for good coverage.

### HOLDING THE STENCIL

Spraying the back of the stencil with adhesive holds each cutout flat to the surface, to stop the dye seeping underneath and blurring the edges of the motif. You can lift and reposition the stencil several times before re-spraying. On fabrics that do not mark, you can hold the stencil in place with masking tape.

## STENCILLING IDEAS

With the same three stencil motifs, you can create an almost infinite variety of designs. Here, a dark paint stands out clearly on a pale fabric when used to create a pattern of crescent moons and large stars, with small stars interspersed in the gaps.

Any item of soft furnishing is a likely candidate for a stencilled pattern. Even simple designs, like a star in each corner of a cushion cover, looks effective. Stencilling another cushion with a moon in each corner creates a complementary pair.

# HOW TO STENCIL ON FABRIC

## YOU WILL NEED

❖ PLAIN FABRIC OR ITEM to stencil
❖ MASKING TAPE OR PAPER CLIPS
❖ OLD FABRIC OR PAPER
❖ CARDBOARD
❖ TAILORS' CHALK
❖ STENCILS
❖ SPRAY ADHESIVE
❖ FABRIC PAINTS
❖ SMALL SPONGE OR STENCIL BRUSH
❖ OLD SAUCER

◀ *For a magical touch of continuity, you can make a laundry bag out of scraps of fabric leftover from making the curtains. Stencilling a row of stars along the bottom edge ties it in well with the other stencilled fabric.*

You can either stencil on the fabric of a ready made item, or if you sew you may find it easier to stencil the fabric before making it up. The basic method for preparing and painting the fabric is the same in either case. Here, a laundry bag is decorated with stars and crescent moons.

**2 Planning the design** Using tailors' chalk, mark the positions of the stencil or stencils on the fabric, allowing for seams and hems as necessary.

**3 Positioning the stencil** Holding the stencil well away from the fabric, lightly spray the back with spray adhesive. Then position the stencil against the marks on the fabric and press in place.

**4 Stencilling the fabric** Follow the standard procedures for painting the stencil. Take extra care to dab all excess paint out of the brush or sponge before stencilling to prevent the paint running on the fabric. To help avoid smudging, leave the stencil in place for 10 minutes to dry, before carefully removing it.

**1 Preparing the fabric** Wash and rinse the fabric or item. Allow it to dry and press it well to remove creases. Stretch the fabric over a padded table or board and hold it taut with masking tape or clips. If there is more than one layer, slip a piece of card between them.

**5 Completing the design** Reposition the stencil to paint the remaining motifs and extra colours. If you are using a different stencil for a second motif, leave the first stencil in place to dry while you paint the next.

**6 Fixing the design** Allow the stencilled fabric to dry overnight, then set the paint following the manufacturers' instructions. With paints that are set by ironing, cover the area with a scrap of clean cloth or iron from the wrong side. Leave the iron on each section for 20 to 30 seconds.

---

## ▼▼▼ TIP ▼▼▼

**WASHING INSTRUCTIONS**
Always check on the washing instructions for the paint before laundering the fabric – or throwing the packaging away.

---

*Stencils are very useful for creating an instant design theme. In this case, gold fleur-de-lys stencilled on a red lampshade link perfectly with red fleur-de-lys on a footstool covered in pure white fabric.*

# STENCILLING FABRIC LENGTHS

When stencilling fabric before sewing, it's important to work out the positioning of the motifs first, so that they end up in the correct place when the item is made up. Remember to allow for hems and seams as well, and for the pattern matching.

You may want to centre a motif, or stencil a border so that it follows the shape of the item – along the leading edge or hem of a curtain for instance. You can test the effect by drawing the outline of the stencil motif on paper, cutting it out and pinning it in place on the fabric.

**1 Marking up the fabric** Measure up and cut out the fabric. Mark the seamlines with chalk or tacking. Lay the fabric pieces out flat and place the stencil on it, moving it about until you are satisfied with the result. Mark the positions of the stencil with tailors' chalk.

**2 Marking up for a border** Measure up and cut out the fabric as before, marking seamlines. Using a ruler and chalk, mark a guideline for positioning the base of the border stencil, taking into account the seam allowances.

▲ *In terms of the spacing and alignment of the motifs, you plan a stencilled border on fabric in the same way as you stencil a border along a wall.*

## READY-MADE ITEMS

It's important to lay ready-made items out as flat as possible. With curtains, ungather the heading so that you can spread the fabric out flat.

❖

For items with a double layer of fabric, such as pillowcases or duvet covers, place a piece of card in between the layers so that the paint does not seep on to the underneath layer.

❖

On curved items, such as a lampshade, use a pliable acetate stencil.

❖

◀ *Stencilling your own designs on fabric is a wonderful opportunity to produce unexpected little touches like the swag of roses on the back of this stripy loose cover. The whole design was created by repeating a single rose and leaf stencil motif.*

# IN PRAISE OF PATCHWORK

*Wherever you use it in your home, patchwork adds texture and eye-catching detail, enriching the decor with its variations of pattern, shape and colour.*

P atchwork was originally devised as a frugal way of recycling old clothes to make warm bed covers, but today it's appreciated as much, if not more, for its decorative value as for its practical advantages. As well as adding colour, pattern and texture to the home, patchwork furnishings have a warm and friendly feel that benefits any environment – from a traditional, country-cottage setting to the most streamlined, contemporary scheme.

There are many ways to introduce patchwork into your home. You can make a small patchwork project yourself – cushions, table mats and tea cosies are quickly assembled from scraps of furnishing fab-

ric; or try your hand at creating a quilt – choose a block design which you can work at your leisure in easy-to-manage sections. Display your treasures cast casually on beds, sofas or chairs or hang a truly magnificent piece in pride of place on a wall.

For instant patchwork furnishings, use one of the many fabrics printed with patchwork patterns that are currently available. Some form part of a coordinated range, so you can repeat the theme with patchwork-print borders, lampshades and so on. Also keep an eye open for patchwork-print crockery and other accessories, and create your own effects with crazy freehand-painted or stencilled patchwork designs.

*Creativity knows no bounds when it comes to patchwork quilts – as this rich and varied bedroom display shows. A bold butterfly-motif quilt makes a dramatic backdrop for the bed, while more softly toned quilts lie across it to balance the effect.*

▶ *Coordinated ranges* of patchwork-print furnishings have almost as much charm as the genuine article. This wallpaper border is from the same range as the curtain and tieback below right.

▲ *Geometric block patchworks*, like the simple square-patch design in mellow beige, cream, olive and black on the wall here, are as at home in modern schemes as they are in traditional, country-style decors.

▶ *A colourful piece of patchwork* can be used in many ways. Here a hexagonal design created from a medley of fabric scraps makes a quirky headboard cover.

▶ *A teatime triumph*, this star-patterned quilt doubles up as a handsome table cloth. It's worth protecting a treasured quilt with a lacy top cloth when you're serving drinks on it.

▶ *For instant patchwork furnishings* use a patchwork-print fabric – this one has a traditional triangular design in fresh, summery florals.

# Guide to Patchwork

**The traditional craft of patchwork is as appealing today as ever, combining design flair with thrifty fabric recycling.**

Patchwork originated from the need to make do and mend – you could call it an early form of recycling. In days gone by, old and worn furnishings and clothes were cut up and restitched together to make bed quilts and new garments. In the eighteenth century, many new patchwork styles evolved when the New World settlers took the art of patchwork from England to America, and the women developed their own methods of piecing and stitching fabrics. Nowadays, both recycling and patchwork are in vogue, though you are more likely to covet patchwork items for your home simply because you like them, rather than for economical reasons.

## Choosing fabrics

As patchwork fabrics need to retain a crease after they are pressed into shape, and be easy to sew, closely-woven, opaque fabrics in natural fibres, such as cotton, fine linen or wool, are the best choice. Avoid synthetic fabrics which are often too slippery to cut accurately, difficult to stitch neatly and hard to press into crisp lines. You can buy packs of assorted fabric remnants for patchwork, but finding your own is more fun. Bear in mind the following points when picking fabrics for patchwork:

❖ All the fabric in one patchwork should be of the same weight and type. The one exception is a style known as crazy patchwork, where the fabric patches are stitched on to a backing fabric.

❖ Make sure that all your chosen patchwork fabrics have the same care qualities, to avoid problems when you come to launder the item.

❖ Avoid mixing old and new fabrics as some will wear out quicker than others.

❖ Be careful with fine fabrics in case the seam allowance shows through to the right side. Either fuse a layer of fine interfacing to the back of fine fabric patches or press the seam allowances to lie against thicker fabric patches.

❖ Before you cut out the patches, wash, dry and press all the fabric pieces to check for colourfastness and shrinkage.

## Materials and equipment

**Beeswax** For handstitched patchwork, first run the thread through a block of beeswax to strengthen it and make it less likely to tangle. Blocks of beeswax are sold in fabric and craft shops.

**Cardboard** Use firm card to make your own *card templates* (1).

**Coloured pencils** Use these to colour in your own patchwork designs, so you can determine the placement of the patches.

**Craft knife and metal ruler** Use a craft knife against a metal ruler to cut out straight-sided cardboard templates.

**Dressmakers' marker pen** (2) Use this to draw around the template on to the fabric.

**Graph paper** A grid is useful for designing and charting your own patterns.

**Needles** For handsewing, use Sharps 9 or 10 for tacking the seam allowance round the paper linings and Betweens 9 or 10 for handsewing the patchwork pieces together. For machine sewing, use a needle which is compatible with the fabric.

**Paper** Use stiff paper, like the pages from glossy magazines, to make the paper linings for hand-stitched, one-shape patchwork.

**Pins** (3) Use fine brass lace pins which don't rust or mark the fabric.

**Rotary cutter and cutting mat** These are useful for cutting straight-sided patches and strips accurately. You can also cut through several layers of fabric at once.

**Scissors** (4) Use sharp dressmakers' shears for cutting out the fabric patches.

**Store-bought templates** (5) You can buy templates for patchwork from craft shops and department stores. They are often sold in pairs. One is solid metal and is used to cut the patchwork papers. The second, which is usually made from plastic or cardboard, is larger by 6mm (¼in) all round to allow for seams, and has a central window so that you can position it over the fabric.

**Thimble** It's a good idea to protect your index finger with a thimble when handstitching patchwork.

**Thread** (6) The main sewing thread should match the fabric type. When stitching a variety of different fabrics together, pick a neutral colour and stitch all the patches together with the same colour thread.

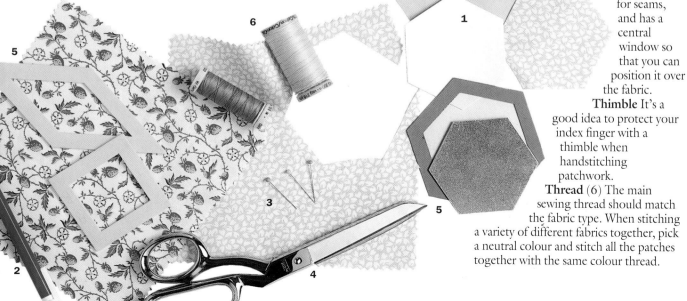

# Patchwork methods

The way the patches are joined together gives each patchwork its character and distinctive style. With careful placement of fabrics of different colours and patterns, you can achieve imaginative and dramatic effects. Sometimes it is easy to see how the patchwork pattern is formed; at other times it can look very complicated indeed.

As a general guide there are two main styles of patchwork, *one-shape patchwork* and *block patchwork*, explained alongside. There are some exceptions to these two groups, involving alternative techniques such as folding or gathering the fabric. A patchwork can also feature appliqué motifs worked in one or many colours.

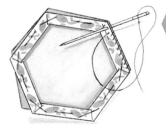

## One-shape patchwork

This is the easiest patchwork to identify as literally all the patches are made from one repeated shape, usually a hexagon or diamond. When worked by hand, the patches are stitched over a foundation of firm paper, which acts as a guide for the shape and also gives the patches body as you sew. The paper is removed when the patchwork is complete.

## Block patchwork

Most styles of patchwork fall into this category. Block patchwork is formed by stitching together squares, rectangles or strips of different shapes and sizes into blocks, which are stitched together in turn to form the finished design. You can form both geometrical or pictorial patterns. This is an ideal way to create large patchwork items, such as quilts, as you can work on one reasonably sized section at a time, and even farm blocks out to fellow patchwork enthusiasts.

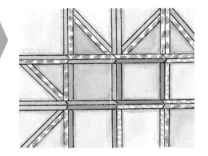

# Glossary of popular patchwork patterns

The nature and immense popularity of patchwork mean that there is a colossal number of recorded, traditional designs. However, there are a few styles, handed down through generations, that are firm favourites and crop up again and again on modern pieces of patchwork – you may recognize many of them.

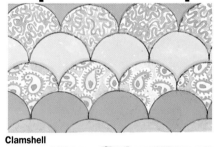
Clamshell

Crazy patchwork

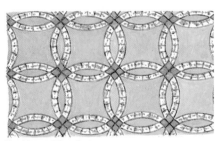
Double wedding ring

Dresden plate

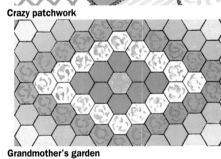
Grandmother's garden

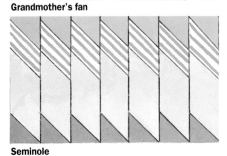
Grandmother's fan

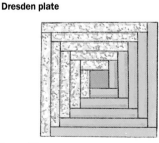
Log cabin

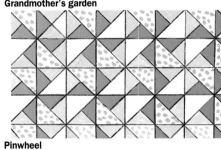
Pinwheel

Seminole

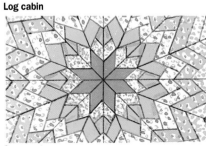
Somerset

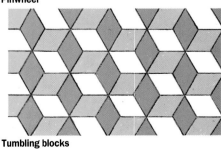
Tumbling blocks

# SQUARE PATCHWORK

*Patchwork soft furnishings are full of character and quickly become treasured possessions. For covetable patchwork with dash, simply machine stitch fabric squares together.*

Of all the patchwork styles, square patchwork is one of the simplest and quickest to work because you can do it all by machine. To achieve success just concentrate on cutting out the shapes accurately and stitching in straight lines. Square patchwork is versatile too – you can cut the squares as big or small as you like and stitch them into a piece of any shape and size, from a huge throw to a dainty cushion.

The fun of creating a piece of patchwork starts when you are choosing your fabrics –

plundering your remnants bag filled with old favourites, rummaging for inexpensive offcuts in your local fabric shop, or attacking discarded clothing with a pair of scissors. Later on your resourcefulness is rewarded and your creativity exercised as you put all your fabrics into the melting pot. The only rules you must heed are to use fabrics of the same weight and type, and not to mix old with new. Otherwise, go ahead and mix colours, patterns and textures to create just the effect you want.

*To create the look of a treasured family heirloom, make your patchwork from pieces of old clothing and furnishing fabrics.*

# GUSSETED PATCHWORK CUSHIONS

## YOU WILL NEED

- ❖ ODDMENTS OF FLORAL COTTON FABRICS
- ❖ 50cm (½yd) PLAIN COTTON FABRIC
- ❖ CARDBOARD OR STIFF PAPER
- ❖ SCISSORS, RULER, PENCIL
- ❖ TAPE MEASURE AND PINS
- ❖ TWO PIECES OF HEAVYWEIGHT (200gm/8oz) WADDING 40 x 32cm (16¼ x 13in)
- ❖ MATCHING THREAD
- ❖ EMBROIDERY COTTON

The patchwork fronts of these pretty cushions are a bright mix of many different floral fabrics, with a plain cotton back and gusset. For sturdy cushions, choose strong, easy-care cottons or cotton mix fabrics. The cushions are padded with layers of thick wadding – enough to give added comfort on sturdy wrought iron or wooden seats. Embroidery thread tufts stitched deep into the cushions give them a welcomingly plump and springy look. The finished cushion measures 40 x 32cm (16¼ x 13in). Take 1cm (⅜in) seams throughout.

**1 Cutting out the squares** Using ruler and pencil draw a 10cm (4in) square on the cardboard. Cut it out. Using it as a template to draw around, cut out 20 squares from the floral fabrics. To plan the final arrangement of the squares, lay them out flat, right side up, and move them around until you are happy with the effect.

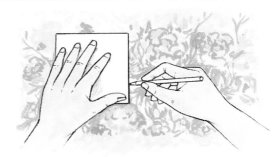

**2 Joining squares** With right sides facing, place two squares together. Pin and stitch, taking a 1cm (⅜in) seam. Repeat to stitch on three more squares end to end, making a strip of five squares. In the same way, stitch the remaining squares into strips of five. Press the seams open.

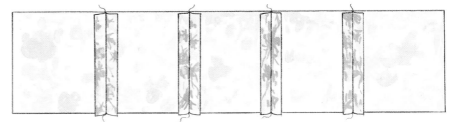

**3 Completing the front** Lay out all the strips in the order you want them. With right sides facing, pin the first two strips together so that the seams match exactly. Machine stitch, taking a 1cm (⅜in) seam allowance. Press the seam open. Repeat to stitch on the remaining strips, forming one piece of patchwork.

**4 Stitching the gusset** Cut a 160 x 6cm (63 x 2¼in) strip of plain fabric, joining strips if necessary. With right sides together and clipping into the corners for ease, pin the strip around the edge of the patchwork so the ends meet at a corner; pin, tack and stitch the ends together where they meet. Stitch the gusset in place.

**5 Adding the back** Cut a 42 x 34cm (17 x 13¾in) rectangle of plain fabric. With right sides together, pin and stitch it to the raw edge of the gusset, leaving a generous opening centrally in one side. Clip into the seam allowances at the corner and turn the cover right side out. Slide in the layers of wadding. Turn in and slipstitch the opening closed.

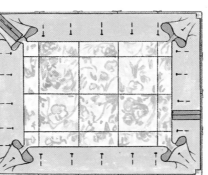

**7 Adding the tufts** Thread a needle with embroidery or button thread and knot the ends. Using the picture as a guide, mark the positions of six tufts on each side of the cushion. Pass the needle through the cushion from back to front. Push the needle through the centre of a tuft and back through the cushion from front to back, pulling firmly. Add another tuft. Thread the needle from back to front two or three times, then fasten off securely.

## ADDING TIES

Cut four 50 x 22cm (19¾ x 8¾in) strips of floral fabric. Fold each strip in half lengthways with right sides together. Stitch along the long edges and diagonally across one short edge. Trim, turn right side out and press. Pleat up the raw ends and pin them to two corners of the back cover piece, before you stitch it to the gusset.

**6 Making the tufts** Cut a 4cm (1½in) strip of card. Wrap the embroidery thread around the card 15-20 times, then cut the thread. Pull the loops of thread off the card. Cut a length of embroidery thread and tie it tightly around the centre of the loops to form a tuft. Make 12 tufts in this way.

*These floral patchwork cushions are great for the garden - they harmonize beautifully with a flowery backdrop and provide a comfy resting place for weary gardeners and sun worshippers alike. Indoors, use the cushions to brighten up a set of dining chairs or a window seat.*

# PATCHWORK SCATTER CUSHION

One of the versatile features of square patchwork is that you can cut the squares into other shapes, such as triangles and rectangles to make more varied patchwork designs. These instructions are for a scatter cushion worked in square patchwork placed on the diagonal and finished with triangles. The back is simply made from plain fabric.

For the best results use four different fabrics for the patches. The cushion has an overlapped opening at the back and measures approximately 38cm (15in) square. Take 1cm (⅜in) seams throughout.

## YOU WILL NEED

- ❖ CARDBOARD/STIFF PAPER
- ❖ RULER AND PENCIL
- ❖ FOUR REMNANTS OF COORDINATING FABRICS
- ❖ 0.5m (½yd) FABRIC for the cushion back
- ❖ SCISSORS
- ❖ CUSHION PAD 38cm (15in) SQUARE
- ❖ MATCHING THREAD
- ❖ 1.8m (2yd) CORD TRIM
- ❖ TAPE MEASURE AND PINS

*Mix plain fabrics in subtly contrasting shades for sophisticated patchwork cushions.*

**1** **Cutting the templates** Using the ruler and pencil draw two 14cm (5½in) squares on to the cardboard. Cut them out and set aside one square (**A**). Cut the second square diagonally in half. Set aside one large triangle (**B**). Cut the remaining triangle in half to make a smaller triangle (**C**). Discard the remaining piece. These three pieces are the templates for the cushion front.

**2** **Cutting out the pieces** Using the templates and adding 1cm (⅜in) seam allowance round each, cut four **A** pieces from the same fabric and one **A** from a different fabric for the centre. Cut four **B** pieces from a third fabric and four **C** pieces from a fourth fabric.

**3** **Starting the patchwork** Lay out the patchwork pieces as shown. With right sides together and raw edges matching, stitch one small triangle **C** to each of the outer squares **A**. Press the seam allowances open. Take two of these stitched pieces and, with right sides together, pin and stitch two large triangles **B** on to each, so that the **B** triangles are on opposite sides of the square.

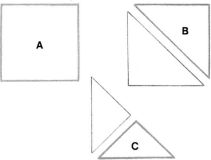

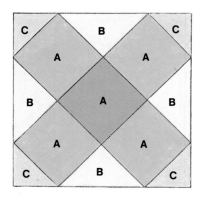

**4** **Finishing the patchwork** Take the remaining two stitched pieces and stitch them either side of the centre square **A**, to form the centre row. With right sides together, pin the three parts of the cushion together and stitch. Press the seams open.

**5** **Stitching the back** Cut two 40 x 30cm (15½ x 12in) rectangles for the back. On one long edge of each rectangle, turn under a 5mm (¼in) then a 1cm (⅜in) hem and stitch. With right sides together and edges matching, position the back pieces on the front so the hemmed edges overlap. Pin, tack and stitch the outer edge. Clip the corners and turn the cover right side out.

**6** **Adding the cord** Slipstitch the cord over the seam all round the edge of the cushion, twisting it into a loop at each corner. Unpick a small hole in the seam, cross over the ends of the cord and push them into the opening. Stitch it closed.

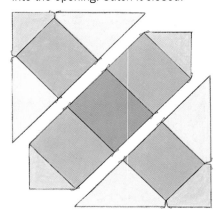

# CANVASWORK

*Canvaswork, petit point, needlepoint – whatever
you call it, hand-stitched, decorative patterns worked on
canvas have a timeless appeal.*

In Victorian times canvaswork was a favourite pastime for ladies of leisure, though it was also a way many an impoverished young woman earned her living. Learning the technique was considered a prerequisite of good breeding, so from a tender age young girls studied it and generously showered relatives and friends with ever more elaborate canvaswork gifts.

Floral motifs, ranging from delicate flowery sprays and ferns to huge, lush cabbage roses in vividly coloured wools, were the most popular designs, but fruit, animals, religious subjects and geometric patterns were also typical. Canvaswork was used to decorate functional items such as footstools, firescreens and cushion covers, or it was simply framed and hung.

Today, canvaswork is valued as a tranquil pastime, offering pleasure in the doing and pride in the finished product. Deciding how to display pieces, whether purely as decorative items or in a more functional role, is part of the enjoyment. Framed canvaswork can be hung individually or grouped; several canvaswork cushions can create an opulent effect on a sofa, while a single large one can make a striking focal point.

If you're new to canvaswork there are complete starter kits available. Try to choose one that matches your decor; you can achieve a modern effect as well as a traditional one, according to choice of design and colour. And if you're keen, there are also clubs and societies to join and adult classes for beginner and more advanced skills.

*An exquisite piece of canvaswork can play a practical as well as a decorative role. With its unusual plaid background and traditional bunch of cabbage roses, this sturdy canvaswork knitting bag makes a lovely old-fashioned feature in a country cottage-style decor.*

**◢ An apple a day** *may keep the doctor away, but this canvaswork shelf edging featuring whole and halved apples is a treat to the eye. Its simplicity has a contemporary appeal — canvaswork needn't always be old-fashioned.*

**◢ Sitting pretty,** *this beautiful canvaswork cushion transforms a hard wooden and cane chair seat into a comfortable one. As a pleasing, long term project, set yourself the goal of making matching canvaswork cushions for a set of dining room chairs.*

**◢ Truly Victorian** *in appearance and appeal, this formally symmetrical canvaswork rug features stylized rhododendrons (another 19th century favourite) in full bloom. Floral canvaswork, cut flowers and living plants are natural display partners, but the time and effort put into canvaswork makes it worth protecting from the damp atmosphere and water splashes that are part of most conservatory environments.*

# Index

## ACKNOWLEDGEMENTS
### Photographs
7 Ariadne Holland, 8-9 El Mueble/Felipe Scheffer, 10(t) Eaglemoss/Simon Page-Ritchie, 10(b) Marie Claire Idées/G. de Chabaneix/C. de Chabaneix/Hamon, 11 IPC Magazines/RHS, 12 Ariadne Holland, 13-14 Ariadne Holland, 15 IPC Magazines/RHS, 17 Colefax & Fowler, 18 Eaglemoss/Graham Rae, 19 Marie Claire Idées/Hussenot/Chastres/Lancrenon, 20 Eaglemoss/Steve Tanner, 21 Ariadne Holland, 23(t) Marie Claire Idées/G. de Chabaneix/C. de Chabaneix, 24(tr) Marie Claire Maison/Snitt/Bayle, 25 Marie Claire Idées/G. de Chabaneix, 26 Eaglemoss/Steve Tanner, 27-28 Eaglemoss/Graham Rae, 29-30 IPC Magazines/RHS, 31-32 Eaglemoss/Simon Page-Ritchie, 33 IPC Magazines/RHS, 34(tl) EWA/Michael Crockett, 34(tr,b)-35 IPC Magazines/RHS, 36-38 Worldwide Syndication Ltd, 39 Ariadne Holland, 40(t) Eaglemoss, 40(bl) IPC Magazines/RHS/Christopher Drake, 40(br) Worldwide Syndication Ltd, 41 EWA/Nick Carter, 43 IPC Magazines/RHS, 44 Eaglemoss/Steve Tanner, 45 EWA/Brian Harrison, 46-47 IPC Magazines/RHS/Blackmore, 48 Crownson Fabrics, 49-52 Eaglemoss/Graham Rae, 53 Marie Claire Maison/Dugied/Postic, 54(tl)

Ariadne Holland, 54(tr) IPC Magazines/RHS, 54(bl) Past Times, 54(br) IPC Magazines/RHS, 55 Ariadne Holland, 56-57 Marie Claire Idées/G. de Chabaneix/C. de Chabaneix, 59 Marie Claire Idées/C. Fleurent/C. Lancrenon, 60-61 Eaglemoss/Graham Rae, 62 Anaya Publishers/Lizzie Orme, 63 Slumberland, 64(t) Tomkinson Carpets Ltd, 64(cl) Dorma, 64(cr) EWA/Tommy Candler, 64(bl) Eaglemoss/Simon Page-Ritchie, 65 Worldwide Syndication Ltd, 66-67 Eaglemoss/Graham Rae, 68 Worldwide Syndication Ltd, 69 Stiebel of Nottingham, 70(l) Sanderson, 70(tr) IPC Magazines/RHS, 70(br) Stiebel of Nottingham, 71-72 IPC Magazines/RHS, 73 Ariadne Holland, 74-75 IPC Magazines/RHS, 75(br) Marie Claire Idées/Hussenot/Chastres/Lancrenon, 76(tr) Marie Claire Idées/Schwartz/Lancrenon/Chombart, 76(bl) IPC Magazines/RHS, 77 Marie Claire Idées/G. de Chabaneix/C. de Chabaneix, 78-79 Laura Ashley, 80-81(t) IPC Magazines/RHS, 81(br) Eaglemoss/Graham Rae, 83(tl) IPC Magazines/RHS, 83-84 Eaglemoss/Graham Rae, 85 Jane Churchill, 86 Eaglemoss/Simon Page-Ritchie, 87 IPC Magazines/RHS/Jan Baldwin, 88 Sanderson, 89-92 Eaglemoss/Graham Rae, 93-94 Eaglemoss/Jonathan Pollock, 95-96 Marie Claire Idées/S.Becquet/C. Lancrenon, 97-98 Marie Claire Idées/Becquet/Faure/Singer, 99-102 Eaglemoss/Steve Tanner, 103-104 Eaglemoss/Paul Bricknell, 105-106 Eaglemoss/Graham Rae, 107 IPC

Magazines/RHS/Christopher Drake, 108(tl) EWA/Neil Lorimer, 108(tr) IPC Magazines/RHS/, 108(bl) IPC Magazines/RHS/Christopher Drake, 108(br) EWA/Michael Crockett, 109(inset) Eaglemoss/Graham Rae, 109-110 IPC Magazines/RHS, 110(br) Eaglemoss/Martin Shaffer, 111 Eaglemoss/Mark Gatehouse, 112 Eaglemoss/Simon Page-Ritchie, 113,114-5(t) Eaglemoss/Graham Rae, 115(bl) PWA International Ltd, 116(t) Modes et Travaux, 116(b) Ariadne Holland, 117 EWA/Lynn Bryant, 118(tl) Ariadne Holland, 118(tr) Marks and Spencer, 118(bl) IPC Magazines/RHS, 118(cr)Ariadne Holland, 118(br) Marks and Spencer, 119-120 Eaglemoss/Graham Rae, 121 Ariadne Holland, 123 Marie Claire Idées/Maltaverne/Faver, 124 IPC Magazines/RHS, 125 Marie Claire Idées/Hussenot/Chastres/ Lancrenon, 126(tl) Marie Claire Idées/M. Schwartz/C. Lancrenon/L. Roque, 126(tr,bl) Ehrman.

### Illustrations
8-30 John Hutchinson, 32 Sally Holmes, 36-67 John Hutchinson, 74-75 Coral Mula, 78-92 John Hutchinson, 93-94 Terry Evans, 96-112 John Hutchinson, 114-115 Coral Mula, 120 Terry Evans, 122-124 John Hutchinson.